Compostelle

Compostelle

The Camino Francès

Or a truly unique pilgrim way

Written and Illustrated by Papychette Howard

Kennedy & Boyd
an imprint of
Zeticula Ltd
Unit 13,
196 Rose Street,
Edinburgh, EH2 4AT
Scotland.

http://www.kennedyandboyd.co.uk
admin@kennedyandboyd.co.uk

First published in 2023
Text and illustrations © Papychette Howard 2023

ISBN 978 1 84921 245 8 Hardback

For my darling Olivia,

For sweet Eve

For Theodore, Maud and Charlie, who brought great joy in our life

Some will say : "Of course God, does not exist".
But I your grandmother tells you:
"God is love and of course He exists as we love each other so much"

Acknowledgements

I could not have realised this book, without the help of my friend Mado. She typed the text and corrected many errors. Spelling is not my strong point!

Then all the friends, who have read the text and gave me some advice, which I followed … or not!

Valentine transfered my drawings on my P.C.

Henry Severac put in place the historical and dialogue texts.

Guy Perdon corrected the last mistakes

Annick Mouillard who encouraged me with her enthusiasm

Peter, my husband who, of course, was in charge of translating the French text into English, and above all my editor Stuart Johnston

Elizabeth Aloccio

Anne-Marie Escobar

Gisèle Candelier

Genieve Palasi

Violaine Lasry

Fanny Berbesson-Joly

Annie Severac

To all, a huge thanks

Introduction

This book is for whom? Not for children - too complicated - neither for adults, too childish. But perhaps for adults who managed to keep their child spirit and particularly those who travelled the Camino.

When Peter and I decided to walk the Compostela Way, we were not in any way sure to be able to make it. We were told that as true Parisians we would not be able to cope with the many privations, lack of comfort and tiredness we would encounter.

But taking up the challenge, we decided to make the journey.

We had both been around the world, yet never have we loved so much a journey as our walk to COMPOSTELA

We had formidable encounters with 'perigrines' coming from different lands, yet despite having shared many joyful and merry dinners we noticed how evasive most were about their deep motivation to go on the pilgrinage.

In 1987, UNESCO, voted the Camino 'The First European Cultural Itinerary'

It is true that the architectural diversity: Romanesque, Gothic, Mozarabe (Christian with the Muslim influence), Mudejar (Muslims working for the Christians), plus some Visigoth ruins and many Roman remains are for those interested an absolute wonder.

Charlemagne and his nephew Roland, Le Cid, Christopher Colombus, Saint Francis of Assisi, Wagner and of course all the Kings and Queens of Spain are mentioned in my tale.

When we returned, I wanted to transpose with my drawings the enchantment I had felt.

But as I recoiled at the idea of exposing my personal feelings, I decided to replace the humans with animals.

I needed for this purpose to give them an imaginary but tragic past so that they would want to make the pilgrimage to COMPOSTELA and turn over a new leaf.

The grey goose was injured by a hunter.

The white mouse was tossed about in a cardboard box, reminding one of the trains going to the concentration camps.

The black cat suffered from racism.

Finally the dog is a political refugee, who had been tortured.

There is also the fox, who represents a person who was sentenced to death in the Middle Ages, and could obtain a reprieve by walking to Compostela.

As for the wild boars, they represent all the hospitals founded for the pilgrims to nurse and protect them from all the dangers they would encounter.

This document remained forgotten in a drawer for more than twenty-five years. The Covid 19 gave us extra leisure time. Consequently with my friend Mado we decided to insert the text with the drawings and we hope our efforts will give you pleasure.

FOR THOSE WHO ARE ALLERGIC TO LEGENDS, GO STRAIGHT TO THE FIRST CHAPTER.

Our stages on the Camino Francès
(Septembre 1994)

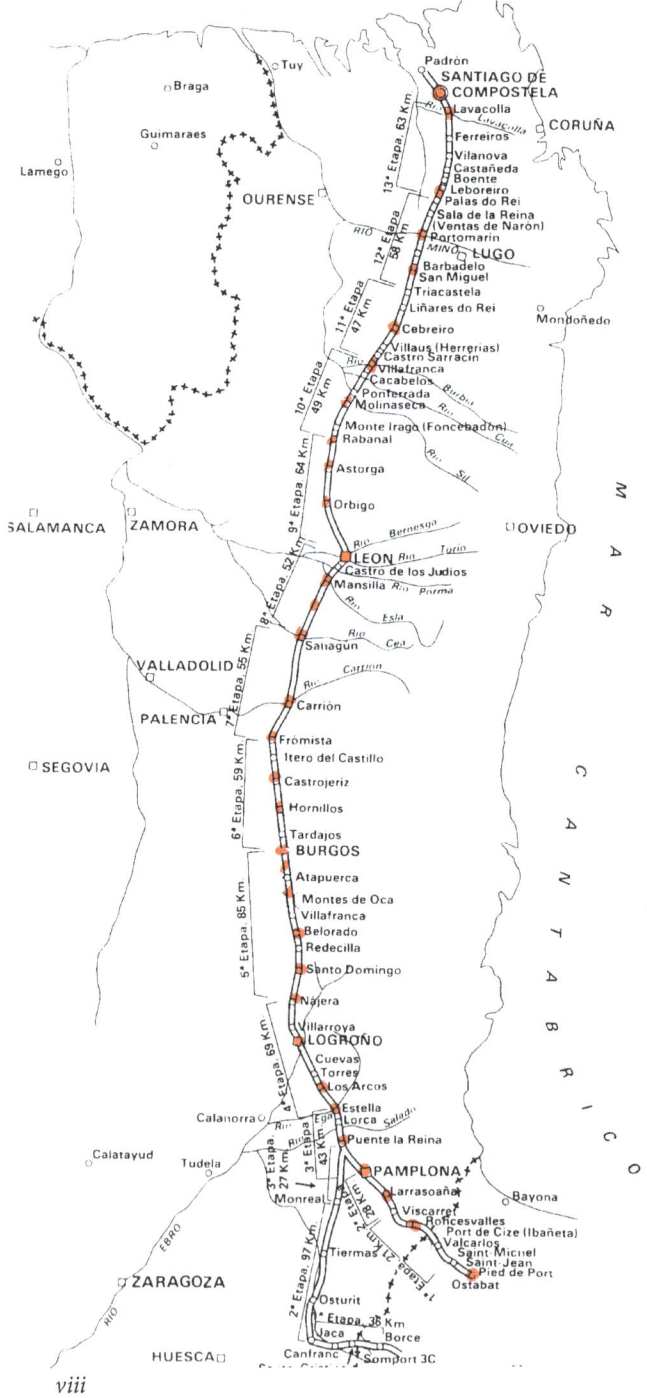

Contents

The Encounter

Ulké, the great wild goose, suddenly moved away, beating her wings.

She could not stand any longer the mind-numbing gossip of those stupid white geese, nor their nasty remarks about the colour of her feathers.

"You are ugly! Your feathers are the colour of dust."

"It's not possible, you have been rolling in the mud"

"My feathers are maybe grey," thinks Ulké,*"but at least I go on long journeys! I am not going round in a circle like those fools! Fortunately my wing is healed! Tomorrow I shall be flying again."*

At that moment, she hears a sob. Surprised, she approaches and discovers, hidden under a large dead leaf, a small white ball which was crying.

"Who are you?"
A tiny mouse looks up at the great goose and says:
"I'm lost!"
"Lost, tell me, perhaps I can help you?"

"I come from Paris where I was happy with my family under the shade of a large chestnut tree. Life was peaceful, until the accursed day when suddenly a man, who had been watching me for a while, grabbed me and pushed me into a cardboard box. It was awful, I was tossed about, upside down in the dark without eating or drinking. When we arrived at the farm I quickly realised that my trials were not over, because when the man opened the box, there was a concert of screams."

"Oh! How awful!"

"It's disgusting!"

"You are crazy! There are already too many on the farm!"

"No way you are going to give this vermin to your son!"

"Tomorrow you must get rid of it!"

"They closed the lid of my box. I was shaking. At night, I made a hole in the lid and fled to the barn where I hoped to find friends. Alas, it was even worse! Thousands of big rats and grey mice gathered around me."

"Oh! He is all white."

"Looks as if he fell into a pot of milk!"

"They screamed, pushing, biting and scratching me, and — I was lucky to run away again... But now I am alone and lost!"

Ulké, the, wild goose, indignant, takes him under her wing and says:

"If you like, I'll take you with me on my trip."

"Hmmm! Hmmm! Please," said a little black cat,"as it happens I heard your conversation and me too, I have a problem because of my colour. Whenever I enter the farm to drink milk with my brothers, the farmer, as soon as she sees me, takes her broom. 'Get out! You dirty beast. Get out, son of a witch!' "

"I do not understand: I am neither dirty nor stupid and my brothers, who are red-headed, have the same mother as me., She named me Amedeo because I reminded her of an Italian painter and also because of a beautiful gypsy friend, —, But it is clear the farmer hates to see my black face! Anyway it is well known that at night all cats are grey! So why make so much noise about my colour?

4

"Be ready tomorrow morning," says Ulkè. *"The three of us will go to see the good Saint James of Compostela. My Great-Great-Grand-Mother says that her Great-Grand-Mother used to tell her he worked miracles and consoled all*

The following morning our three friends start their journey. They go towards the big forest where Ulké knows of a good refuge. Julius Cesar, the little mouse, drunk with joy to have escaped all those grey mice runs from left to right, jumps from a rock to a pebble, despite what Ulké says.

"Don't run like that. You must keep your strength, the refuge is still far away!"

But the little mouse listened with only one ear. To this day he has only known his cage and the cardboard box and he enjoys his new freedom.

Amadeo is fascinated by the stories that Ulké tells him and wants to know where the great traveller comes from.

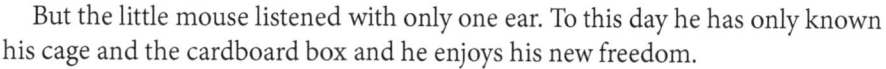

"You may not understand," explains the wild goose. *For the time being, the place is covered by snow.*
"Snow?"
"Yes, it is beautiful but everything disappears under it. That's why we leave every year after the autumn."

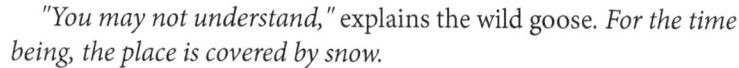

"Oh! you are so lucky to have travelled so much..... I have never left my village."
"Well, you will see many villages, all very different along The Camino of Compostela."

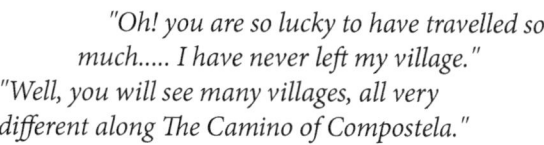
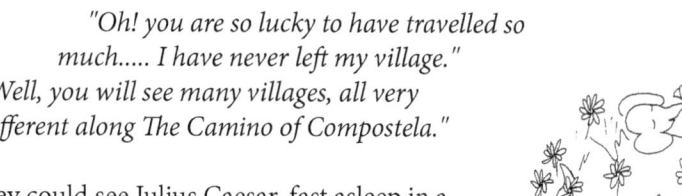

They came to the top of a hill where they could see Julius Caesar, fast asleep in a field of daisies, a blue butterfly on the top of his nose.
"I knew," said Ulké,*"that he could not run like that all day."*

"Let's stop like him, but not for too long, because you see our refuge is in the forest where my friend, the fox, lives."
"A fox? Did you say a fox?"
"Are you afraid?"
"Ahem.. It is...."
"Look! Julius Caesar is a mouse and you are a cat and still you are friends! Be careful not to be influenced by other people's gossip, and make your own judgement."
Ashamed, the litle cat then said to her:
"You are right, we shall accompany you."
When they are both well rested, they wake up Julius Caesar.
"What? How? Already? I am still very tired. My legs can't carry me me anymore. Cannot we stay a little longer?" he says, begging.
"No. Our refuge is still too far away."

With a deep sigh Julius Caesar rises. He doesn't jump anymore on one pebble to another. He walks straight ahead, barely noticing the flowers and a butterfly in his path.

Paris seems far away, and he misses the comfort of his family's cage. He doesn't know anymore whether he wants to travel to Santiago de Compostella. It might be too far for a little mouse?

Amedeo immediately guessed what was on his friend's mind.

"If you want, climb on my back, my legs are bigger than yours.
  We will go to see the fox."
"A fox?"
"Don't worry, he's Ulké's friend."
"I am glad you trust me. You will be surprised by Theodore the fox."

They feel their tiredness disappear, eager to know Ulké's friend.

The sunset soon touches the top of a splendid leafy dome of oak and chestnut trees. Wild rabbits play in the shade and are leaping everywhere, squirrels chase each other in the trees, a mother hedgehog leads her family for a walk. It is beautiful and calm.

"It is like being in a church," said Julius Caesar.

"Follow me," says Ulké, who knows the forest very well.

They arrive at a ravine overlooking a large river.

Theodore the fox is there, and at his side stands a hen, a cock pheasant, a wild boar, a large hare, a jay, a dove, a magpie and a multitude of other inhabitants of the forest such as snails, ladybirds and dragonflies.

A rabbit steers Theodore's attention to the travellers.

"By God! But it's Ulké, my great friend! How happy to see you! But how come you are so late? Your whole family came through a long time ago. I was worried about you."

"I had an accident- a hunter's bullet delayed me. But I don't regret it, this has allowed me to make good friends."

"Come, come! Ulké's friends are my friends. We are holding a "forest council", with all the wild representatives, to see what improvements we could make. But you must be tired. Go and rest. Tonight we are going to have a dinner party."

Julius Caesar whispers to Amedeo:

"We were right to trust Ulké!"

The little cat answers thoughtfully :

"We should thank the evil farmer, because our situation seemed desperate, but thanks to her, we are living an extraordinary adventure."

"So right you are. It shows you must never lose hope," says Ulké.

In the evening, they sat comfortably on soft foam seats around a fire of crisp logs.

After the delicious nettle soup, cereal pasta, desserts arrive in abundance. Everyone had made either a blueberry pie, a hazelnut cake, a raspberry ice cream, including delicious blackberry wine, lime blossom, wild thyme and marjoram herbal teas – in short a real feast.

By popular demand, Theodore was compelled to tell his life story. It didn't bother him, because he now likes to talk, and hopes to convince those who still have doubts.

"*Here, a long time ago, this corner of the forest was sad and dirty. Deserted by all. No bird songs, no rustling or insects, the rabbits were hiding. It was complete desolation. I lived there all alone! I spent my life killing and strangling. I had no pity for anyone: women, children, everyone. The madness to kill more and more had possessed me. My den was crowded with corpses, feathers were rotting, everywhere it smelled of death and misery. I was mean and always angry and very unhappy. Nobody wanted to talk to me, or approach me and this loneliness was driving me crazy. One day however an old hermit, who lived on the other side of the river, came to see me.*"

"*Hello, Fox!*
"*I grunted something like: 'How dare you disturb me?'*"

"*It's because I have observed you for a long time – you are killing more than is necessary. Everyone runs away from you and you are not happy. You take and never give. If you want I can help you to change your life.*"

With a groan, I replied :
"*In what way does that concerns you? My happiness or misfortune!*"
"*Happiness should be everyone's business . We depend on each other. Look at the forest around you, how sad it is. If you promise me not to touch my friends, I'll send a turtle dove to show you the way.*"
"*After he left, I stood there circling around my den like a beast in a cage, bumping into bones. Old rotten carcasses. It was hardly pleasant! Even me, I thought it smelled bad. Suddenly I was sickened by all the blood I had shed. Why not go and see the hermit, thought I? It does not commit me to anything.*"

" When the turtle dove came, I followed her," recounts Theodore, suddenly very moved, looking around him.

" You were all there, his friends, and later you became my friends as well."

The animals nodded, smiling gravely, saying:

"Yes we were there; we were afraid of you, as your reputation for cruelty had crossed the river. But the hermit asked us to trust you, and since we couldn't refuse this good man anything, we all came over."

"My life was transformed. I was so surprised that I could talk to you without you running away. Then the squirrel came with a hazelnut cake and the mother rabbit a carrot cake. It was too much. I burst into tears. Then the old hermit told me: 'You see how much better it is to receive than to steal, and believe me it is even better to give.'

"Hermit, tell me what I must do to live amongst you. I never want to go back to my dark den ever.

"You must repent, Fox, my friend. You have done too much harm around you. Go on the road to Compostela to think about it, and ask Good Santiago to help you."

"Upon my return, I was sad not to find the hermit. He had died. But he had said I should replace him."

"Theodore, we are also going to Compostela. Can you give us some advice and useful addresses?"

"Sure! I have made plenty of friends and above all I have the equipment you will need. Let's go to sleep. Tomorrow, we have a lot to organise."

It's the little mouse who was happy to go to bed –
all these adventures were very tiring.
After breakfast, they discovered Theodore's treasure.
There was absolutely everything you need to make the trip.

Ulké hesitates a lot between two hats, to finally take none at all - they are a tiny bit too big.

Amadeo tries all the walking boots. With a sigh, he decides he has already too many legs to be bothered by them. Yet it is a regret as he finds them very pretty.

Theodore, helped by Julius Caesar, prepares a First Aid box.

"Very important," he says. *"You must have: some sweets for the throat, an elixir of perlimpinpin for the feet, some powder for fractures! Alas I have a terrible stock. Honey candies and fruit jellies - very good, for the morale, when at the bottom of a hill.... you will need it."*

Poor Theodore, he would have liked to accompany them, but he had too many responsibilities towards his forest companions.

At the end the Fox says worriedly

"My friends, I must warn you that there will be several dangerous times during the trip – lands, inhabited by packs of wolves which, alas, are as ferocious, as I was once myself. Fortunately, I am friendly with the wild boars of the region, and I will send a messenger for your protection at night.

"Thank you so much," says Ulké. *"Now it is time for us to hit the road."*

"Come in my arms and give me a kiss," says Theodore, hiding his tears of emotion.

"Thank you, thank you again," shout Amadeo and Julius Caesar, turning around every three steps.

"Farewell and Buen Camino!"

They have been walking for several days without any problems. Amadeo was mocking Julius Caesar, with a bag almost as big as himself.

"You won't go far with that load!"
"Maybe, but you will be very happy to share its contents. I have a million good things in there to erase tiredness."
"Yes, but if walking with this heavy bag makes you tired, you would just as well walk without it," he said mockingly.
Ulké laughs.

Suddenly Amadeo stands up.

"Don't you hear cries for help? Moans? Quick, it's on this side, lets go!"

They came to a large tree to find a dog who was half-dead and terribly thin, attached to the trunk.

"Water, water to drink!"

They were petrified by this scene of horror, Ulké finally recovering her senses says:

"The first thing to do is to untie him!"

"But how?"

"Julius Caesar, can you gnaw this rope?"

"I am too small!

"I have an idea," says Amadeo.,*"Get on my back."*

"I still can't make it!

"Wait, I am going to go piggyback, and now?"

"Get on your tiptoes."

Finally, Julius Caesar grabs the rope and begins to gnaw it furiously, so the rope gives way and the poor dog falls at their feet.

Ulké quickly opens the gourd and makes him drink.

"Julius Caesar, it is the moment to open your bag and offer this poor dog some food."

Julius Caesar throws a triumphant look at Amadeo, and then looks for all the best things he has at the bottom of his bag.

"No, No! Just a little bit, he is too weak, we must be careful not to give him too much. Go, both of you, and make a stretcher with the rope. We shall carry him until he can walk."

No sooner said than done! They pile their bags on the stretcher and delicately place the dog. Amadeo goes in front, Ulké behind, Julius Caesar leads the way pointing out large stones and roots which could cause them to trip. Ulké says, concerned:

"It is tonight that we will cross the land of the wolves. Let us hope that Theodore hasn't forgotten to warn the wild boars, because our invalid would be in real danger!

When she had finished speaking, Julius Caesar finds himself face-to-face with a crow, who says:

"Hello, the boars have asked me to show you the way. From here you take first right, then at the oak tree you turn left, at the poplar tree you go straight on until the chestnut tree. There you turn left... No, I am wrong! There you turn right."

Ulké interrupts:

"Couldn't you lead us yourself? We are very tired and we have an invalid with us."

"No problem, just follow!" says Arthur.

Arthur, the crow, delighted to help, leads them straight to the clearing of the wild boar. Amedeo is surprised.

"I do not understand; we haven't turned once to the left or to the right!"

"Oh, that was the way for tourists, us locals we go straight!, and you said you were tired;

"Thank you so much," says Ulké. *"You see I am not used to travelling on foot. It is so less tiring for me to fly. I shall be pleased when we arrive."*

"Here we are. There is the chief! I must warn you, he is very hard of hearing. It makes him grumpy. But you can't get a better Chief! The wolves are terribly afraid of his temper. With him around you will fear nothing tonight."

Leon, the old chief, greats them gruffly:

"You are late. I have been waiting for you for two hours. What do I see, you are four? Ah! I must have misheard again. I am becoming so deaf," he grumbles.

Fortunately, his wife, Leontine, had prepared enough chestnut purée for an entire regiment.

"Go and wash in the stream, have a rest and we'll call you for dinner."

After having entrusted the dog to Leontine, our three friends take a well-deserved foot bath. Ulké wiggles with pleasure. That water is refreshing. What a pity the stream isn't deep enough for a swim! Amedeo carefully dips the end of his foot in the water and removes it immediately, while Julius Caesar says to Ulké:

"I would love to know how to swim like you."

"I will teach you; its important. Now let's go to see how the dog is doing."

They go straight to the infirmary that Leontine, the mother boar, had immediately set up.

"How is he?"

"His leg is broken and the skin on his neck is badly damaged. He still doesn't speak. He is too weak."

"I shall need a lot of 'bone powder' for his fracture."

"We could ask Theodore, he has a terribly large stock", said Julius Caesar,"I even believe that he would be happy to get rid of it."

"I think so," says Leontine. "That reminds him too much of his former victims!"

"I, can go now, if you wish," says Arthur. "If I leave now, I'll be back in four strokes of a wing, and I'll bring you the powder before midnight."

"But how are you going to do it during the night?"

"Oh! I have a lot of owl buddies, who will guide me if I lose my way."

"Thank you so much for the poor dog," says Ulké. "We still do not know his name, but we already like him a lot."

"Don't forget, straight ahead!" howls Julius Caesar to Arthur, who takes off.

"See you tonight," he croaks.

They make a big fire. The evening is wonderful., After the delicious chestnut purée, accompanied by a fricassée of mushrooms sprinkled with wild mint and the dessert of small hazelnuts coated with honey, they decide to wait for Arthur's return and play the game of snakes and ladders. Guess who wins?

"This is not fair, Ulké. It is too easy for you," said the fat Leon, for once howling with laughter. "I offer you a revenge match, but this time you will play the wolf and I the sheep., I warn you I am unbeatable. Come on, children, take a lesson. If you want to become an old boar like me, you have to know how to hold the wolf at bay."

Leon was indeed winning, when suddenly they hear:

"Here he comes! Here he comes!"

Arthur, with a great rustling of wings, lands close to the fire.

"Phew! I really thought I couldn't do it. It is terribly difficult to fly with a bag around your neck. I almost gave up. But when I thought of that poor dog, I thought to myself: they are all counting on you – you must succeed!, and here I am."

Leontine grabbed the bag and quickly mixed the bone powder in a glass and gives it to the dog, who drinks it all.

"Thank you," he whispered quietly and immediately fell asleep.

"We shall do the same. Arthur - if you wish to sleep around the fire with the others. We shall guard you, so that you can sleep in peace."

It took a week for the dog to recover. He told them his name was Pietre, speaking very quietly so as not make much noise.

He did not tell them anything about his misfortune nor the reason why he had been found half dead, tied to a tree. They noticed that he did not want to talk much about it.

"It is too early," said Leontine – he should not be questioned.

So everybody left him alone.

Later when he was able to walk on crutches, they decided to start again on the Camino to their first stop: Saint-Jean-Pied-de-Port.

"Tomorrow, we will sleep in Saint-Jean- Pied-de-Port," explains Ulké. *"I have often flown over it., It is so pretty seen from the sky, I am thrilled to be able to see the town at last. This is the official beginning of what is called:* **The Camino Frances"**

They have to walk slowly, because of the poor dog. They are happy and proud, knowing that the passport they will receive at Saint-Jean-Pied-de-Port will make them proper pilgrims.

"Courage! Come on. It is at the top of the street that Madame Debril will hand us our passports."

The cobbled street with large irregular stones was very difficult for Pietre with his crutches. They are finally very happy to arrive, but Madame Debril is not happy at all and let them know it.

"Phew! I can't take anymore," says Pietre, collapsing, in the grass.

"Open your bag, Julius Caesar, it is at moments like this that it will help to recover our strength."

"Pilgrims, you call yourselves, and you want me to believe you? You are surely impostors! Brigands, thugs. You only want this passport to have a free holiday. But I am not fooled. You do not know me. I will not fall into this trap."

"Madame Debril," said Ulké, trying to stop her. *"We want to walk to Santiago de Compostela. We are true pilgrims."*

"No way. You can try at the monastery at Roncevalles, with the monks there if you want, but I am sure they will refuse."

In a curt tone, she tells them to leave and closed the door with a big key, despite the fact the refugio was empty.

"Did you see that she didn't even notice our pilgrim shells," said Amadeo angrily.

Pietre didn't speak. He was very disappointed. He needed so much to rest, but was used to bad luck. Ulké, who felt responsible for the group, said :

"Come along, we will sleep near the walls of the castle and whatever Madame Debril says, we shall go to Roncevalles!"

Once well settled, they dine with the provisions of the bag. Amadeo asks:

"But how shall we recognize the Path?"

"We're going to follow the route of the Milky Way, and we won't be the first!"

"What do you mean?"

"It is said that Charlemagne had a dream: Saint-Jacques appeared to him and asked him to drive the Infidels out of Spain, then go to pray at his tomb."

"But how shall I find it?" asked Charlemagne."Follow the route of the Milky Way, at the end of the path, you will find my grave there."

"And he did?"

"He went to Spain with his nephew Roland to hunt the Infidels, and it was on his return from one of these battles that Roland died. Don't worry, pilgrims have been following the Camino Francès for more than a thousand years, and everywhere you will see yellow arrows or scallops on the walls of houses, on the trunks of trees, on large stones, on bridges. Everywhere: You can't go wrong. More than a thousand years!"

Ulké adds:

"Kings, queens, monks, warriors, beggars, saints and sometimes even repentant brigands, many, many people have passed on this path. You will see, it is really not a path like any others!"

And here is what our four pilgrims will discover along "THIS PATH REALLY UNLIKE THE OTHERS": Roman roads, ancient bridges, pretty churches, dream landscapes, Spaniards, people from all over the world, in short: "The CAMINO".

Stage 1: SAINT-JEAN-PIED-DE-PORT to RONCEVAUX

The next day they set off early in bright sunshine. It is indeed a splendid day. The mountain is magnificent, but very steep, and the path goes up and up and they stop frequently to drink from their gourds. At last they arrive at the Ibaneta pass, out of breath. There is a statue of the Blessed Virgin, surrounded by clouds. She appears to be waiting for them.

"Phew! I can't take anymore," says Pietre collapsing in the grass.*,"Open your bag, Julius Caesar, it is at moments like this that it will help to recover our strength."*

Amadeo , who was jumping around, suddenly stops.

"Look, there is a sword on that big stone. What does that mean?
"It's in memory of Roland, Charlemagne's nephew," replies Ulké.
"He died here?

"Yes, in August 778, surrounded by twelve valiant knights."

"Why didn't Charlemagne come to his rescue?"

"He was far below in the valley, and when he heard Roland's elephant horn, it was too late."

"When Roland realised he was going to die, he tried to break 'Durandal', his cherished sword so that no one could use it after him."

"Oh! When I think I'm in the very place where Charlemagne may have trod, I feel quite weird," says Julius Caesar.

That makes Ulké laugh:

*"Charlemagne was a great Emperor who once ruled most of Europe. Being a devoted Christian, he built monasteries and churches on the route to Compostela or the 'Camino Frances' as it is known in Spain. He would have been delighted had he known that the Camino was named in 1987 : **The first European cultural route.** "*

"For more, than a thousand years, pilgrims have travelled the Camino, Frances. You will be guided by yellow arrows and St Jacque shells everywhere: on walls, tree trunks, large boulders – absolutely everywhere: you can't go wrong. Over a thousand years," says Ulké thoughtfully and adds:

"Kings, queens, monks, warriors, beggars, saints and even repentant robbers – so many pilgrims have been on this route. You will see it isn't like any "way" you would have known."

Ulké had noticed the dark clouds clinging to the summit. The once beautiful view had disappeared, replaced by thick mist. The path was even more difficult on the descent. It was now raining and drops were dripping down their noses and necks. They are blinded and can no longer see the beautiful beech forest, and are unable to know where to set foot — tree trunks seemed to be following each other indefinitely.

"We are going to get lost in this fog," moans Julius Caesar.

"I'm exhausted," said Amadeo.

"I'm getting frozen," grumbles Julius Caesar.

Pietre does not say anything. He grits his teeth bravely.

"I have flown over this forest many times. We have just to follow this stream. It will lead us to Roncevalles … Look! we can see the roof of the monastery already."

They arrive, muddy and exhausted by the long walk and shivering with cold and fatigue, but Ulké doesn't allow them to rest.

"Let's go to see the monk for our 'credentials'!"
"I am afraid! What if he doesn't want to give them to us?"
says Amadeo.
"Precisely; let us not waste time."
The monk receives them with great kindness.

"I am not used to see pilgrims like you, he said looking puzzled, but you look brave and honest. I will give you the 'credentials', so that you can continue all the way to Compostela. I do hope you arrive there, in good health. But do not forget to pray for me.
To-night you should attend the service and the blessing for the pilgrims.
Meanwhile, go to the dormitory and take a nice hot shower – it seems you need it!"

All clean and warm, they go to the church. The superb stained-glass windows sparkled in the last rays of the sun. They were immediately attracted by the silver statue of the virgin, who holds the baby Jesus in her left arm, and a bouquet of precious stones in the other. A great Archangel with outstretched wings seem to watch over and protect the mother and child—

"She is so beautiful," whispers Julius Caesar, *"but she looks sad! "*

At the same time, the procession of monks arrive and the blessing for the pilgrims begins in several languages. Ulké giggles, she laughs so much she hides her head under her wings to stifle her chuckles. She only just succeeds saying to her neighbour, Pietre:

"They are not very gifted at languages, the brave monks!"

The next morning, they visit the museum of the monastery. Pietre is determined to see the well-known chessboard, sculptured in crystal, which once belonged to Charlemagne and said to contain pieces of Jesus's crucifixion cross.

"Do you realise that this chessboard is over a thousand years old?"
They then proceed to the tomb of Sancho II, El Fuerte.
"It's incredible how tall he was!"
"He was 2.25 m tall!"
"I do feel so small," says Julius Caesar, *"and what are those big chains?"*
"He brought them back after his victory over the Moslem king in 1212 at Naves de Tolosa. This victory was so important that it is incorporated on the Navarra coat of arms. Now finish – sightseeing over. Have you forgotton the Camino?"

While Amadeo, Julius Caesar and Ulké are getting ready, Pìetre went away discreetly.
"Where has he gone?

Everybody is looking for him. He comes back without his crutches.
"I left them in the church, in front of child Jesus."

Stage 2: from RONCEVAUX to LARRASOANA

Taking to the road again, Ulké explains:

"We are now in Spain and we shall give the Spanish names to the towns and villages we visit. We are in the Basque Country, in the proud province of NAVARRA."

The sun is shining and the countryside is beautiful. Everything is so green and the farms well kept. There are trout in the rivers, jumping out of the water to wish a 'Buen Camino' to our pilgrims.

"Pffuit. I have already drunk everything in my water bottle, and I am still thirsty. The sun is scorching," growls Amadeo.

"We are going to stop in the village of BURGETE, where we will ask for water," says Ulké.

The village is superb: one large street, bordered by houses with wooden doors embedded with shining copper studs. Carved stones are encircling them. The coat of arms tells the title of nobility of the ancient owners. If one sees one or more scallops, it means that they have also made the pilgrimage to SANTIAGO DE COMPOSTELA.

"Shall we stop here?" suggests Ulké.

Pietre sees that the door of one of the beautiful houses is partly open. He takes the opportunity to ask for some water from the lady watering her plants.

"With pleasure," she says,*"and here are some dried figs from last year. I can see that you are not used to walking under the blazing sun, and these will give you strength.*

"Keep going, we will soon be there!, Look at this pretty house next to the old bridge and also the old church, on which there is a stork's nest. One of my friends usually stops here," says Ulké. *"I will check if she is still there. I will go and see,"*

But the nest is empty.

"It's a pity," says Ulké, *"but as we have our 'credentials' we are going to go to the 'Refugio', as they say in Spanish."*

The mayor of LARRASOANA with the predestined name of Santiago Zubiri Elizade welcomed them heartily to his village.

"Fantastic, fantastic! my friends! Come to my office; I want to take a photo of you." He is very pleased; this photo is going to join all the paper cuttings, signatures of celebrities and souvenirs of the Camino.

Laughing, he said *"I too have made the pilgrimage to Santiago, with a name like mine, I could not have done otherwise! The friends of The Camino have made a book about the pilgrimage, of which we are very proud.*

Give me your credential, so that I can stamp it with the seal of LARRASOANA. Now you are free to go to the refugio."

Despite a splendid hot shower, they feel very cold, being the result of their arduous long walk. Julius Caesar's sack was empty *"I am so hungry,"* he said.

In the refugio, pilgrims, coming from all over the world, were getting ready to go to the nearby restaurant.

"Come with us," said two Spanish boys. *"We will help you choose from the menu."*

They feel shy to share the table with other pilgrims, but that is the magic of the Camino; they are welcomed by everybody as if there were no apparent differences.

The boiling soup arrives, with tender white beans and crispy bits of bacon – it is delicious. Our four pilgrims sigh with pleasure. They don't dare to try the 'vino tinto', but their companions have already attacked several jugs. The ambiance is one of joy and gaiety. As they have no money, their fellow pilgrims pay for them.

"'Viva el Camino' says Pietre, going to bed.

"Tomorrow Pamplona," says Ulké, yawning.

"Sleep well as we shall be up early."

Stage 3: from LARRASOANA to PAMPLONA

The sun is already high in the sky, when Ulké wakes up her companions.

They cross the bridge on the river Arga again, being the river that will accompany them to PAMPLONA

"I am quite pleased about it," says Julius Caesar. *"I love listening to the sound of flowing water – it makes a, charming song and this river is particularly beautiful. Look at all these minute golden brown frogs, no bigger than the nail of your thumb. It is incredible, they are everywhere!"*

Stopping, Julius Caesar starts a conversation with one of them.

"I don't know if I can take you with me."

"No, it's not possible," says Ulké. *"We are going through large areas where there is no water, and it would be too dangerous for her."*

The little frog was terribly disappointed and is nearly crying.

"But if you wish, we can meet at PUNTA LA REINA, where I shall give Amadeo his first swimming lesson."

Full of hope, the little frog wishes them a super Camino.

"See you soon then!"

"Now , lets go to PAMPLONA!"

"Do you know, Julius Caesar, it, was, a great Roman general who founded this town, a century before Christ. His name was Pompée."

"Pompée, Pamplona ..."

"Pompée - POMPLONA has often been destroyed. Even Charlemagne tried to pull down the fortified walls which he found so menacing. It was on returning from one of these expeditions that the poor Roland, his nephew died."

"After the Romans came the Visigoths, followed, by the Moors."

"It was the kings of Navarra who governed the country. Around the year 1000, Sancho III, El Mayor who reigned from 1004 to 1035, planned the actual Camino from Pamplona to Santiago. It is thanks to him that we are here today. It was his distant descendant who was fighting the Moors, and who is buried in Roncevalles.

SANCHO EL MAYOR

They have at last arrived in Pamplona, in front of the town hall, adorned with majestic lions on its balcony. Without a word the four of them imitate the glorious attitude of the lions.

The inhabitants are very surprised. They are used to seeing all sorts of pilgrims, but as strange as these – never.

It is quite evident that Amedeo's imitation is the best, helped by his leonine profile!!

They pass the statue of Sancho El Mayor.

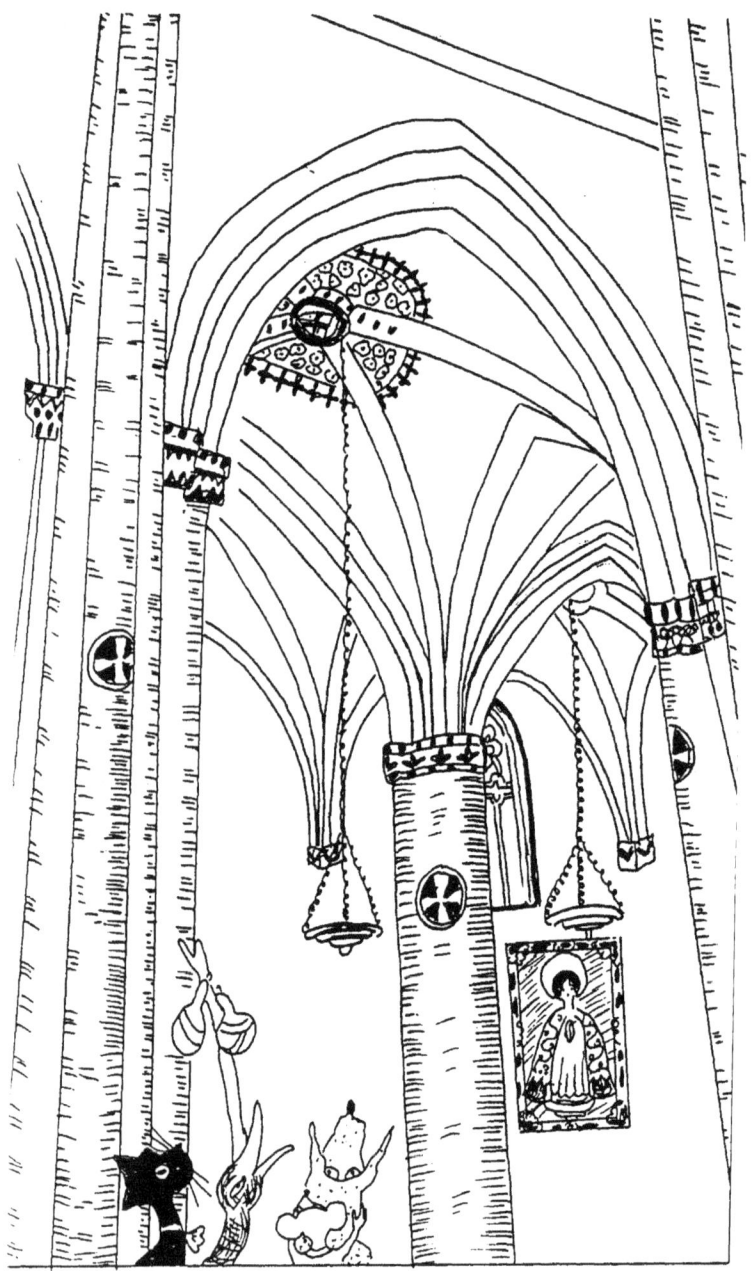

In the cathedral they stop in front of the tomb of the King and Queen.

"They look so peaceful and the their little dog so contented to be along side them!"

Then they look up and are amazed by the height of the nave, encrusted with several coats of arms.

They stop in front of the sculptured wooden main altar, relating scenes of the bible.

"Oh! How terrible. Those cruel men with their daggers killing small children."

"But look at the top, there is the statue of St Jacques."

"All the same," mutters Pietre shivering,*"it brings back so many bad memories.*

"They are capable of being so cruel these men. I want to leave."

"Straight to the citadel," says Ulké. *"I have a surprise for you."*

They are pleased to leave the busy streets, where everyone looks at them as if they were circus animals.

"One would think that they have never seen foreign pilgrims," mutters Pietre, who, without his crutches, feels very tired.

At long last they are at the park, under the big trees. There are flowers everywhere and, in the distance in a dark green area, one can see the profile of a little wall seemingly made of stone lace surrounding, a moat filled in with grass.

"I am going to speak to the Grand Cerf, as he is the chief and no doubt he will ask us to stay the night."

"Ulké, my good friend. It is such a great pleasure to see you. Your sisters came a long time ago. I was going to send ducks to scout around for you as we were worried."

"Many thanks, but you see, here I am with good friends."

"Go down into the moat, before the guardian arrives."

There are many sorts of animals, even white geese, who are by no means stupid. On the contrary, they immediately surround Ulké, asking her a thousand questions and giving her the latest news.

"We are preparing The Fiesta of San Fermin. Could you not stay a little longer? It is such a jolly fiesta."

"We will come back another year. Tomorrow we are off to PUENTA LA REINA," answers Ulké.

The dog missed all this – he was already asleep.

"We should do the same. The route is still long. Many thanks for the dinner, Grand Cerf, and good night."

Stage 4: from PAMPLONA to PUENTE-LA-REINA

The dog having had a good rest, they leave very early the next morning.

After a long walk under an unmerciful sun, they see before them a small octagonal chapel, encircled by arches in the middle of a cornfield.

"Let's stay here a moment," suggests Ulké. *"We could picnic under the beautiful tree."*

Pietre and Ulké visit the chapel. A soft light, through the alabaster window shines on to the altar, on which stands a gold wooden statue. A pilgrim is deep in prayer. They leave discreetly.

They find Julius Caesar and Amadeo looking up into the sky.

"Oh! But these are peregrine falcons. You are right to be frightened, Julius Caesar. There are no better birds of prey. In the middle ages the noble lords used to hunt with these peregrine falcons."

"Eh, you up there, would you like to picnic with us?"

Julius Caesar is not reassured. In a second the falcons are diving on them at a frightening speed. Dying of fear, he hides in his big sack, and everybody laughs at him. He eventually sticks his head out of his sack, a little ashamed.

"Don't be frightened, little mouse. We have seen that you are pilgrims. You have nothing to fear."

Feeling reassured, he gets completely out of his bag, holding a piece of chorizo in his hand.:

"It's for you," he says, and they lunch happily together.

"You are lucky to have meet us," said the peregrine falcon," *because before you arrive at BURGOS you have to cross a very dangerous area: LOS MONTES DE OCA. It is a place which has the reputation to have many ferocious wolves. In the middle ages, pilgrims were very anxious to pass through this area, because bandits and packs of wolves were hiding in the forest. But do not worry, we will keep an eye on you until you are out of danger."*

After, warmly thanking the peregrine falcons, it is time to take to the camino again.

At the end of the day, they finally reach PUENTA LA REINA, where a beautiful bridge is mirrored in the River Arga.

"You will be delighted, Amadeo - this is where you are going to have your first swimming lesson. But first we must have the stamp on our credentials."

The refugio is huge, lines and lines of beds, three high in a vast cool room.

"Brrr! It's not very pleasant here!" says Amadéo.

"It belongs to the monks," replies Ulké. *"I would be surprised if their bedrooms were more comfortable.*

They cross the town through the Calle Major- a very narrow street through which filters rays of sun. On the balcony, balls made of copper shine amongst the bright red geraniums.

"One can be thankful to the Queen who built this bridge in the 11th Century for the pilgrims. She was probably the wife of Sancho el Mayor or maybe she was Queen Estafania de Najera – nobody really knows.

Deep down, Amadeo doesn't care. He doesn't want to thank any Queen. Above all, he does not want to go the river. But unluckily for him all the children are there. He does not want to be rediculous.

"Let's go! Amadeo, I shall start with you!"

Amadeo reluctantly gets into the water. Large red fish try to cheer him up, but for the moment you can see he is not attracted to aquatic sport!

Julius Caesar, becoming impatient, copes with Pietre and the frogs. Pietre knows how to swim, although his style lacks elegance. It is effective and that is quite sufficient.

In the evening, the church bells are ringing. They go to mass and, if some meditate, the others are rather drowsy after the emotions of the day. A gilded wooden statue of Saint Jacques seems to smile at them. The priest, noticing the presence of pilgrims, gives them a special blessing for the Camino.

As soon as their dinner is finished, they immediately go to bed, exhausted.

Stage 5: from PUENTE-LA-REINA to ESTELLA and to IRACHE

Leaving early, the town is sleeping. The streets, which were so busy and crowded the night before, are now deserted, with the restaurants and bars closed.

"I could have done with breakfast before leaving," sighs Julius Caesar.

"We will find a bar open on the way," says Ulké.

The Camino is splendid. They enter the province of ... NAVARRA;

Wild flowers brighten up the steep hillsides: Camomile, corn flowers, poppies, bluebells and golden grass ripple in waves in the sweet morning breeze.

They take a deep breath.

"It is great to be out so early in the morning," says Amadeo, who had difficulty in getting up this morning.

After a while they lose their ardour, and they are walking more slowly.

"You don't realise we never stop – going up and down all morning – my legs are hurting," says Pietre!

" We can stop," says Ulké, trying to be understanding. *"We can rest our feet in the stream, as it is safe here, not like the RIO SALADO."*

"The first guidebook of the Camino, written in the Middle Ages by a French pilgrim called Amairy Picaud, tells us that the RIO SALADO was poisoned by cruel Basque bandits. They cut up the poisoned horses with huge knives and took the purse bags from the poor pilgrims, who were too ill to defend themselves."

"You frighten me to death with your stories. You surely needed to be very courageous to walk the camino at that period!"

"Courage! We only have to climb up this hill and we shall be well rewarded, at the top is the village of CIRAUQUI."

"In fact, if you look down at your feet, you will notice we are walking on regular flagstones. These are remnants of the Roman Empire. You see, the first Julius Caesar came to Spain. And, CIRAUQUI became an ancient Roman city."

"You mean that CIRAUQUI is an ancient Roman town, and that Spain was under Roman law?"

"Gaulle, England, Macedonia, Greece – in fact from the Tiber to the Euphrates without forgetting the Danube, all these countries were once under Roman Law.

"The Romans built so many roads, there is a saying 'All the roads lead to Rome'. If initally these roads were built for military reasons, they have helped merchants, travellers and pilgrims like ourselves."

They visit CIRAUQUI hurriedly as they must be in ESTELLA before nightfall.

"ESTELLA? It is like Compostela – the city of stars?"

"During the Roman period it was called GEBALDA, then under the Moors it was LIZARRAI. It is said that in 1805 there was a miracle – Shepherds saw the image of the Virgin of Notre-Dame-du-Puy in a myriad of stars.

The king Sancho Ramirez had at the time decided to enlarge the town as a halt for the pilgrims who went on the Camino, inviting the French pilgrims to remain to help fight the Moors. In 1492, King Jean d'Albret decided to harbour the jews who had been expulsed from the province of CASTILLA, then in 1512, King Ferdinand of Aragon captured NAVARRA and destroyed the castle of ESTELLA, and half the cloister of the beautiful church, which we will visit later."

"Oh, Ulké, I'm getting lost with all these kings!

"At that period, Spain was not as today a united country. Nearly all the provinces were independent kingdoms, and the kings were spending their time fighting each other."

"As in France?"

"It was just the same all over Europe."

"But Charlemagne had unified all those countries with his Empire?"

"It did not last very long. When he died, his sons quarrelled... and the Empire was finished."

"Look, we are in front of San Pedro de La Rua, the very church that had its cloister destroyed. Let's go and have a look."

Julius Caesar stopped in front of a huge stairway – completely demoralised.

"You are not serious, Ulké. You are not suggesting we go up these steps at the end of a tiring day. Go without me!"

"Courage," says Amadeo. "I'll wait for you."

"No, no, I cannot, and anyway I am too hot!"

"Come on," says Ulké impatiently. "We will take a bathe later in the Fountain of LOS CHORROS, before we visit the royal palace."

At these words, the little mouse gets up, sighing loudly and joins her companions, They are admiring the magnificent portal of the church.,

"You could say it is made of lace", says the little mouse, out of breath.

"Yes, the Christians spent their life combating the Moors, but more than once they have copied their style."

They pushed open the heavy wooden door. Inside in the choir, a tall Christ is surrounded by two graceful statues, an archbishop with his golden mitre, and a beautiful Virgin.

"She is so lovely," whispers Amadeo.

"Her smile is so tender and she seems to hold an apple in her hand. Her child is smiling as well!

"Jesus lifts his finger. It is certainly to indicate that we should listen to him."

"Look at this extraordinary pillar," says Amadeo, who was sneaking around. "It looks like a braid of hair, but it is in fact made of stone."

"Come into the cloister, you will find others as strange as this one."

"It is a good thing 'your' King of Aragon did not destroy it all," says Julius Caesar, "who feels revived by the coolness of the superb cloister, where identical pillars are succeeding one another."

"Identical?"

"Not really, some tilt in a bizarre way."

They leave the church, and, go into the Royal Palace and Ulké calls them.

"Come and look by the window! There is a splendid view of San Pedro from here. Look at the capitals with their fantastic animals."

"The, most famous is the one of Roland fighting the giant Ferragut."

"Roland? The same Roland?"

"Who is the giant Ferragut?"

"He was a Moor, a remote ancestor of Goliath. He was thirty-six foot tall and as strong as forty men! No dagger or sword could penetrate his skin, but the gallant Roland with his famous Durandale pierced his navel, being his only weak spot."

"Look – you can see Ferragut falling off his horse."

"Ah, I wish I could meet this Roland," sighs Amadeo.

"Me, it is Ferragut, the giant as strong as forty men!"

"Stop arguing," says Ulké. "Let's take a well-earned bathe in the fountain of Chorros."

Julius Caesar has his revenge, as he is the first in the water. Amadeo still does not like water. He is feeling thwarted, but Pietre is sorry for him, and, uses his shell to cool him down.

"Now that we are all dry and cool, we shall not remain in the town, as there is no refugio here, but do not worry as I know of a place where we can go."

They go towards the Carcel bridge, which makes a large arc over the river EGA., There are sheep crossing, slipping and falling on each other – it is an infernal stampede.

"Who built this bridge?" bleats the ram in an authoritorian voice. *"Such a sheer slope is idiotic ...Oh men!"*

"Come on sheep," says the ram. *"Behave yourselves! Looking at you, one would imagine it is the first time you cross a bridge."*

Ulké goes to ask him:

"Is the monastey at IRACHE still under repair?"

"Yes, and it will be a while before it will be finished.

"That's good, we will go and sleep there when the workers leave."

"But the doors will be closed," says the ram.

"I know, but I will drop my pilgrim staff and will fly inside."

"How practical wings are," says the ram. *"If we had wings, we would not have had such trouble with the bridge."*

They pass in front of the church of Saint Sepulchre, with its sculptured facade – on one side the crucifixion and on the other the last supper. On each side of the main door there are statues: one of a now forgotten bishop and the other Saint Jacques, making a superb scene in the setting sun.

Now walking along San Nicolas street, they leave the town by the Portal of the Castille and after a short walk find themselves in front of the closed door of the MONASTERY OF IRACHE.

Ulké drops her staff and, flapping powerfully her wings, flies very high in the sky then descends inside the monastery, and opens the door as promised.

"Phew! It's good to fly again, after all that walking – I was wondering if I still knew how to fly."

Her three companions do not feel so much at ease.

"You mustn't worry," says Ulké. *"Before the monastery became a well known university, it was initially a hospital for pilgrims, even earlier than Roncevalles so it is more than normal for us to take refuge here."*

They make themselves as comfortable as possible and are soon fast asleep.

In the morning when the workmen discover them, it is such fun, as they are surprised to see pilgrims out of the ordinary, and decide to take them for a tour of the church.

The church is not only huge but white and luminous with ornate capitals depicting centaurs, flowers and strange animals. The immense pillars which are supporting the dome are terminated by large shells.

"I have never seen Saint Jacque shells as large as these!"

"IRACHE has more surprises for you!"

The workers, very pleased with their enthusiasm, tell them to go and see the monk's fountain. In saying this, they slap each others backs, finding it all very funny.

Very intrigued, our pilgrims go down to the fountain, and to their surprise find two taps: one for water and one for.... wine! Accompanied by a notice: Help yourself 'sin abusar'.

"What does it means?"

"It's now or never," says Pietre, *"we ought to try!"*

Ulké, for once, does not know what to do.

"Let's try the wine," says Pietre impatiently. *"It is the monks themselves who have invited us."*

They fill their gourd to the brim; taste a little and then taste it again and again.....

"Hmmm – not bad."

"Have another drink!"

"Really delicious," says Pietre, pursing his lips.

The gourd is almost empty.. They fill it again and leave for LOS ARCOS.

44

Stage 6: from IRACHE to LOS ARCOS

They start walking merrily, as the sun is not too hot, and the Camino at this time of the morning is beautiful. They feel happy and then suddenly Julius Caesar says:

"I do not know why, but my legs are very heavy and I feel I only want to sleep."

"For me, it's my head," says Amadeo … *"I feel really queer."*

"It's probably because we haven't had breakfast. Let's stop and open our bags."

They are in a golden field and butterflies fly from flower to flower. An old olive tree provides shade. They start to eat.

"I'm really thirsty," says Pietre. He drinks heavily from his flask.

"It's funny," says Ulké, *"but I can hardly stand up straight."*

She is all askew and with her long neck tries to find some equilibrium.

"Oh! You look incredible that way," chuckles Amadeo.

With infectious laughter, Julius Caesar says: *"I see double."*

They all roll on the ground, bursting with laughter.

"When I think of that horrible farmer's wife back home. It's thanks to her that we are travelling the world."

"Hiccups! Excuse me," says Julius Caesar.

"Think of that blood-thirsty hunter. It's thanks to him that I met you."

Pietre laughs so much that it is impossible to understand what he says.

With a giggle, Ulké says:

"I think we should have a nap ; the wine of the monks was delicious but it does produce strange effects."

Pietre snores very loudly, but nobody notices. They all sleep; they are dead drunk.

After the siesta, they are all a bit ashamed and decide, to make up for lost time.

On arrival at LOS ARCOS, the church is closed, but anyway they are too tired to visit anything. Their heads are still heavy and to quench their thirst they go to the fountain.

"I have never found the water so good," sighs Pietre.

"Neither have I," they all repeated one after the other.

After having their credentials stamped, they are directed to a small disaffected school, which is used as a refugio. Most of the pilgrims had already left for dinner, but there remain only four vacant beds left in a small room. With the morning experience still weighing on them, they go straight to bed.

The other pilgrims return, making a terrible noise.

It must be the "vino tinto", they thought to themselves, expert in the matter!

Two Spanish boys are snoring so loudly that Julius Caesar feels his bed shaking. Impossible to sleep, they pick up their things and leave on tip-toe. It will be better outside, and the moon lights up the path.

"Here – it's perfect," decides Ulké.

The following morning, they are awakened by a group of partridges. They look around them, only to discover that they are in a cemetery of milestones. On one of them is marked 'Compostela 682 miles'.

Stage 7: from LOS ARCOS to LOGRONO - VIANA

The sun is shining, but there is a strong wind. This does not help Ulké; the soles of her feet are very swollen. Julius Caesar is very tired, because he did not sleep well in the field, and the wind doesn't help. Ulké would love to fly, but she doesn't want to abandon her companions as they do not know the "Way".

At long last after a long day of suffering, they arrive in LOGRONO.

In a turning before the city, an old woman, as wrinkled as a parchment, stops them.

"Halt! You are entering the REPUBLICA AUTONOME of LA RIOJA. I am the guardian of the frontier. You must put your name and address in my book."

Very keen to adhere to the rules, Julius Caesar is trying hard with his writing, but it doesn't look very good.

"Could I do a drawing instead?"

The guardian is thrilled – she has four new names in her book, and she offers them some succulent and very sugary figs.

"Do you know you are in the region where the Matamoro appeared?"

"Who is the Matamoro," asks Pierre?

"Saint-Jacques-Matamoro, killer of Moors. The King Ramiro, the first of Leon and the Asturies, refused to deliver the tribute of a hundred virgins that the cruel Caliph was demanding every year, and this resulted in a huge battle. But Ramiro was not afraid because the night before Santiago had promised in a dream to drive the infidels out of the country. Consequently in the morning of the battle of Clavijo in 844 he advanced, full of ardour, shouting: 'Ahead – with Santiago'."

"And then?"

"Of course, he won!" says the old woman, shocked by such a question.

"The Caliph never had the virgins as a tribute anymore."

"The Matamoro, what was he like?"

"Superb, confirms the old woman proudly. *"All alone on a huge white horse and armed with a holy cross and his big sword, he himself killed sixteen thousand infidels."*

"Pfuit! That's certainly more than Julius Caesar," says the little mouse with admiration,*"and he was assisted by his army."*

While telling her story, the old woman had noticed that Ulké and Julius Caesar were visibly suffering.

"You should go to the hospital. They are accustomed to receiving pilgrims."

"That's a good idea," says Pietre, who was helping Ulké.

On arrival at LOGRONO, they make straight for the hospital.

"Ah! I see, I see," said the doctor. *"It is essential to rest for a day, put some ice on your feet, take these pills, and then you should be O.K."*

The nurse who gives them a dressing says:

"This is great, as tomorrow there is FIESTA in VIANA. If you wish I will take you there after my work. Meanwhile, you should visit LOGRONO's cellars, which have such a reputation."

Ulké and Julius Caesar feel already much better. In La Rua Vieja they stop in front of a fantastic representation of Santiago Matamoros.

"I can understand that he frightened the Moors."

They walk slowly to the cave.

"Be careful with the steps," says the patron. *"I am going to let you taste my best vintage wines."*

They enter a beautiful vaulted cellar, full of huge barrels.

"Here, taste this one, and let me know what you think."

"Be very careful," said Ulké in a soft voice. *"Remember the saying 'Taste in moderation! We now know what that means!"*

They select a good bottle to thank Trinidad, their nurse, who, during the, journey by car to VIANA, described the history of her city.

"VIANA was founded by Sancho El Fuerte in 1219. It was a frontier town with CASTILLE, and you can still see the old fortified walls."

"There is a very famous person buried here, Caesar Borgia, who died in 1507. He had committed so many crimes in his country that he was obliged, to, leave. His tomb remained in the church for many years. In the last century the bishop thought it scandalous that this cruel and treacherous man was buried inside the church. His tomb was, consequently moved on to the square in front of the church so that people could walk on him, to show their disdain."

The next morning they join in the celebrations in VIANA. All the inhabitants participate. The men, women and children are all dressed in white with red scarves, berets, belts and the girls with red flowers in their hair. It is the Fiesta.

In the streets young bulls are everywhere and everybody runs away laughing. There are cardboard giants menacing children with their whips, making the children flee in every direction.

When our four friends saw the giants they looked at each other without speaking and decided what to do.

And hop!, Pietre jumps on Ulké's wings, Amadeo on Pietre's shoulders and Julius Caesar on the top. The crowds roar with delight!!

Later in the arena, Ulké, Trinidad and
Julius Caesar admire the prowess of Pietre and
Amadeo, both dressed as the inhabitants of
Viana.

Amadeo is careful, but Pietre is fantastic– it
would appear he has challenged bulls all his life!

The crowd is over excited – screaming Olés
and Vivas, throwing flowers, applauding, its
delirium.

In the evening, at the superb banquet
everyone wants to invite them. The good Rioja
wine flows freely, yet they are very cautious
as they will be back on the Camino the next
morning.

Stage 8: from VIANA to NAJERA

The sun is shining. Trinidad told them that it was in this province of Abelda de Uruega, around the year 900, that for the first time in Europe arabic numerals were used in the monastery of San Martin.

"Arabs? What Arab numerals?"

"Before that, people used Roman numerals. It was more complicated, and also the Romans did not have the number zero. Zero is an arabic invention, and from its use the science of mathematics developed a lot."

Still walking, fascinated by that story, they arrive in NAVARRETE and decide to have a good breakfast. While the other three were dipping their croissants in the cup of chocolate, Ulké continues to recount :

"It was here in 1367 that a valiant French Knight, who was helping Henri II Transmatare, was taken prisoner by the Black Prince, but as he was such a brave knight, the King of France paid a heavy ransom to recover him."

With breakfast finished they climb the steps to the entrance of the church of the Asuncion, and having put in a coin to see the altarpiece the choir lights up revealing the beautiful paintings.

"Oh, such wonders, with all the scenes from the Bible painted in rich colours," exclaims Amadeo, overwhelmed.

Having admired everything, they walk on the Camino again - in silence to assimilate all the beauty. Eventually NAJERA looms in the distance. They follow a long wall on which is written a Spanish poem: "Peregrino, quien te llama?"

"What does it mean?" says Julius Caesar.

" 'Pilgrim, who is calling you?'"

"You are very lucky to speak Spanish so well. I would like to learn as well. In fact I already know how to say 'Queso'."

"'Queso', what is it?"

"Cheese", answers Julius Caesar proudly.

"It is true that it is a survival word for a mouse," jokes Amadeo.

"Stop teasing, hurry up, we have so much to see in NAJERA. Did you notice those large red rocks? That is where you will find Santa Maria la Real. In fact part of the church is carved into the rock.

Legend has it that King Don Garcia, who was also called El de Najera was hunting a poor dove with his peregrine falcon. When the two birds disappeared into the interior of the cave the king followed them and found them sitting side-by-side in front of the Virgin., He was so moved, that he built a church around the cave."

"I'm getting tired."

"A little more effort – we can soon rest in the Knight's cloister. You have surely never seen anything like it. The style is 'plasteresque', because the sculpture is so fine and delicate that it is reminiscent of the silver dishes of the period."

"What date was it built?"

"The sixteenth century."

It was a great pleasure for them all to sit down, when they entered the cloister.

"We have been walking nearly 40km, sighs Julius Caesar. *"It's a long way for my little legs."*

Ulké, to prove that the palms of her feet were completely healed, flew and landed on a column in the middle of the cloister.

The others admired the stone lace sculptures – little angels playing with wolves, strange animals, fantastic birds, men in prayer...

"It's true, Ulké, that we have never seen anything so beautiful."

"Wait – You have not seen yet all the wonders of Santa Maria La Real.

We will now go to the see the Pantheons of the kings of Navarra. This is Dona Bianca's tomb, who died giving birth to Alfonso III, King of Castille. The little child who flies away represents the soul of Dona Bianca."

"Yet you told us it was the pantheon of the Kings of Navarra."

"At the beginning it was, but in 1076 the Province of La Rioja was attached to the kingdom of Castille., In fact the very first coin of the Reconquest, which has been found, was minted here in Najera for King Sancho The Great."

Leaving the church with the stamp of the town on their credentials, they are very surprised by a strong wind.

"Too bad – I was thinking of taking you to an island on the Rio NAJERILLA, but instead we must find the refugio.

We can have a late night, because tomorrow we will be walking less than usual."

"Fine," says Amadeo – *"a little lazing around will not be unpleasant.*

Stage 9: from NAJERA to SANTO DOMINGO DE LA CALZADA

The following morning, they climb a steep slope carved into the rock that overlooks the church Santa Maria La Real. They are in the middle of a pine wood with fine sand on the ground.

"We are just missing the sea!"

They are confronted by an impressive vineyard.

"You have the Rioja wine in front of you," announces Pietre, in a grandilioquent manner.

A terrible wind is blowing over the vineyard! They are all bent double and silent, struggling with all their might against the wind. Ulké looks like a dragon with all her feathers ruffled.

Suddenley, Pietre, who takes the lead to protect Julius Caesar, hears,

"Damn! Damn!"

"What did you say?" asks Pietre, believing the wind had distorted his words.

"I said Damn. Ulké said we would have a relaxed little walk, and in fact I have never been so exhausted in my life."

"Let's sit down," says Ulké .

In the vineyard, there are ripe bunches of grapes.

"Do you think we can taste them?", says Amadeo.

"Well! I am going to taste some, announces Julius Caesar, biting a huge grape. *"It is a matter of survival. I must get my strength back."*

Pietre and Amadeo do the same. Only the virtuous Ulké resists the temptation. After a while, feeling somewhat ashamed of their theft, they return on the Camino.

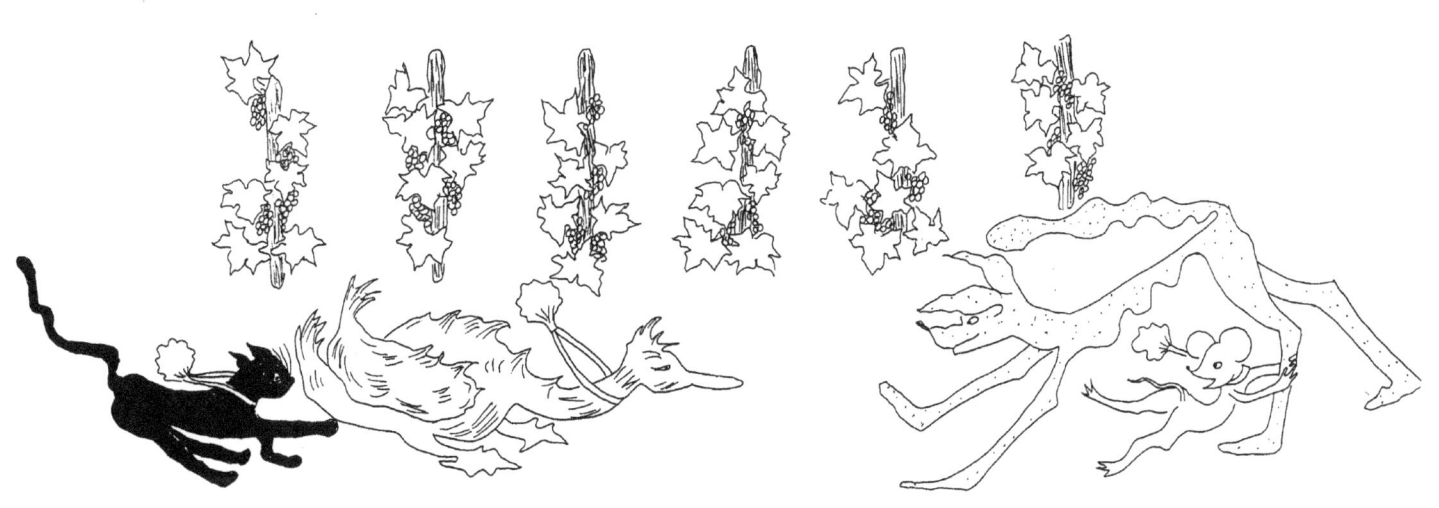

"Oh! Watch the cyclist. It is so funny," says Julius Caesar in a better mood. *"He pedals with all his might, but doesn't move an inch, and even going downhill."*

"Yes, wind is even more treacherous for cyclists than for pedestrians."

They arrive alongside the cyclist.

"I believe," said Pietre, laughing,*"that this man is saying the same thing as Julius Caesar, but in Spanish!*

Finally after a continual struggle against the strong wind, they can see the tower of the cathedral.

"Let's go to the refugio straight away – it is among the best of the camino. It is run, since the middle ages, by the same Family of The Brotherhood of Saint Jacques.

Seeing them arrive, the hospitaleros exclaims:

"Madre des Dios! Pilgrims like you. It's almost a miracle! Go and visit the church, you will meet other friends there," he says, laughing.

Indeed, inside the church, they stopped, not believing their eyes, Ulké laughs at their astonishment.

"It's abominable to be be locked up like that," growls Pietre, very angry.

He throws the rope to the top of the chicken coop, in which are enclosed a white rooster with a superb red crest and plump hen.

"Quick, Julius Caesar, Climb and deliver them."

"I am coming to open your door, Mr Rooster and Madam hen."

"No way. In what way are you meddling," asks the rooster, very angry – his crest bristling. *"We have a week to go and nothing will stop us. It is such an honour to be chosen."*

"Honour, chosen, what do you mean," asks Pietre, dumbfounded.

"We are proud to continue the tradition," replies the rooster, puffed up with pride. *"We are the same family, from father to son since the middle ages, and we are still here."*

"But how is that?"

"A miracle" repeats Pietre, more and more lost.

"How ignorant you are – the miracle known as the 'hanged man unhanged', of course. Go back and look at the painting above the door, which explains everything."

The four of them sit near a pretty balustrade, in front of the door and listen to the rooster who recounts the story.

"There was once a father, mother and a young boy, who were making the pilgrimage to Santiago de Compostela. They were in an inn, where the servant, finding the young man very handsome, wanted to seduce him. But he was pure and innocent and didn't understand and rejected her advances, The servant, vexed and angry, put a cup of silver in the boy's pocket, crying out:

'Thief; Thief! This boy has stolen a cup of silver.'

No one believed the boy when he denied having taken the cup. He was hanged."

"Oh! Poor boy."

"She is lucky not to be around, that damned servant," growls Pietre.

"Wait, wait," says the rooster – *"the story is not finished. When the sorrowing parents, returning from Santiago, wanted to have a last look at their child, they went to the gibbet, and what was their surprise when they heard their son say: 'Mum and Dad, I am alive. The good Saint Jacques held up my feet, when you were away. Untie me'."*

"The parents ran to the judge, who was seated in front of a capon and roast fat hen. When the parents told him that their son was alive, he laughed and said: 'As alive at that roaster and that hen!' "

"At this very moment the roaster and the hen leap up from the platter, fully fledged and started crowing and cackling."

The judge, amazed and ashamed of his mistake ran to rescue the boy. The nasty liar was hanged in his place.

"Justice is done," they all said together.

"And since that day, we are present in the church to recall the miracle," said the hen, chuckling with pleasure.

"It is unfortunate that you see the church during the restoration, because we have the most beautiful altarpiece in Spain - I mean in the world. We have heard of the one in Seville, with its two thousand characters, but I am sure its does not reach the beauty, the elegance, the fantasy, the lightness of the work of Master Damien Forment. This renaissance sculptor came to SANTO DOMINGO DE LA CALZADA with his whole family for twenty years and died during the night of 24th December 1540."

"I am sure he went straight to heaven," said the rooster gravely. *"Fortunately his nephew , who was his assistant, was able to continue his work."*

"Why is the altarpiece not there?"

"A fire, a terrible fire!"

"We thought were going to be roasted like our famous ancestors," the hen replies with a chuckle of restrospective fear.

"But do not forget to see the tomb of Santo Domingo, which is next door in the small crypt."

They visit the tomb of this saint, who was an important builder and protector of pilgrims. He built this magnificent church and restored many bridges and the roman roads to fascilitate the passage of pilgrims.

When they return to the refugio, everyone is waiting impatiently for them.

"Have you seen the hen house?"

So they recounted what they had seen. The other pilgrims could not be more astonished.

"We are really in the city of miracles,", muttered an old Swiss man under his breath.

Stage 10: from SANTO DOMINGO DE LA CALZADA to BELORADO

The following morning, the sun is still shining, but the wind has not completely stopped. The main road has replaced the ancient camino.

Julius Caesar, not naturally very patient, grumbles again:

"These lorries are mad – they are going to crush us! A speed like that should be forbidden. It makes me feel ill and I feel rather sick.

"True," says Pietre,*"They should have made a path for pilgrims next to the road. It's dangerous."*

At the end of a tedious day, they arrive exhausted at BELORADO.

Julius Ceasar feels sick. Amadeo has tummy trouble. Pietre as usual does not complain but looks grey.

"Fortunately I have my friends, the storks who roost every year on the church. They will help us," says Ulké, alarmed by the sick condition of her companions.

58

WC

"Go and see Barbara, she is the hospitalera of the refugio. She is German – we often stay in her town every year in Germany – she will help."

In fact Barbara is really charming. She immediately takes them up a small rickety wooden staircase towards the unique bed of the refugio.

"I keep it for the sick."

Suddenly Pietre rushes downstairs.

"Quick! The toilets!"

In the evening, they receive the visit of the local priest. Smiling, he asks :

"Did you try the grapes? Very often tired pilgrims grab a few, but it is a mistake, because the winegrowers wary of theft spray a product on their vines. It is better to wait until they give some grapes to you. The Spanish are very generous."

"It's my fault, I tempted them all," says Julius Caesar, feeling very ashamed.

"Oh! It's not very serious," says the priest. "Tomorrow morning you will feel better. I will bring you some hot croissants and you will be able to start again on the right foot."

They were, however sick, all through the night. Above their bed is a dark and, gloomy painting of a bare-footed monk surrounded by human skulls.

"Brrr!, Not very comforting, this picture," says Pietre, returning from the toilet for the tenth time.

"It makes you think of the vanity of life," answers the little mouse. "Adios, my friends, I feel I am about to die."

Fortunately, Barbara is there and she is so kind.

"Come on now – tomorrow you will be better, and if you still feel frail you can stay."

Thanks to Barbara, they stay longer. They go to thank the priest in his beautiful church, Santa Maria. Going out in the sun they find there are many women surrounded by mountains of peppers of many different colours. Nearby, a fire is on. Amadeo, who loves colour, cannot resist and proposes to help and a few minutes later the four of them are putting peppers in jars.

"Don't touch the red one – you will have your mouth on fire. Enough of gastronomique experiences for the time being," says Amadeo, rubbing his tummy.

Stage 11: from BELORADO to SAN JUAN DE ORTEGA

"Oh! I am so pleased to leave those skulls behind," says Julius Caesar who had been very impressed. 'Viva la Vida' he hums with true happiness to be alive.

"Today, we shall climb the MONTES DE OCA. The mountain is covered by a beautiful oak forest. This is an area that so terrified the pilgrims during the Middle Ages, because ferocious packs of wolves and bandits were hiding there, and the pilgrim was never sure to be able to arrive at SAN JUAN DE ORTEGA. During the winter, snow and blizzards that you know well made conditions very difficult. That is why San Juan de Ortega built a hospital and a church to protect the pilgrims."

Julius Caesar looks up at the sky and waves his arms in the air.

"These brave peregrine falcons have kept their word. They are protecting us in the forest as they promised. It is, agreable to feel protected. Why do we not ask them to lunch?

At their call, the peregrine falcon dives on them at great speed. Despite a feeling of fear, Julius Caesar holds his ground.

The falcon congratulates him.

"When I think of all the risks pilgrims were taking in earlier days I feel ashamed."

"It is true, said the falcon, *"that there were so many different types of people on the Camino – great ladies with their servants or prisoners serving their sentences. There were more or less honest pilgrims who traded their services and walked the pilgrimage for the old or ill who were not able to carry out their vows themselves. One could never know who one met."*

"I am very happy not to be living in the middle ages and I can profit from this wonderful forest, listen to the song of the skylarks rather than the howling of wolves and admire these little mauve flowers, which are so pretty. One could that say that the path is covered with stars."

"These are wild crocuses and they will accompany us all the way to Santiago."

"Now we must leave our friendly falcons and the Province of La Rioja to enter Castilla."

They continue until they see the beautiful outline of the church of San Juan de Ortega and enter the church.

"What I prefer in the Romanesque churches are the carved stone capitals used in the middle ages to tell the stories– they are as beautiful as an illustrated picture book."

"Look at this one - Jesus in his cradle held up by an angel while the donkey and the ox warm the child with their large muzzles."

They admire the tomb of San Juan.

"The whole history of his life is told here . He died in 1162, but it was much later in the fifteenth century that they added his sarcophage in the church."

"I love these alabaster windows which give out a magic light."

"They are even more magical than you think, as on the 21st of March and the 23rd of September, being the equinox of spring and autumn ...."

"What do you mean?"

"The architect, maybe San Juan himself, managed to design the church so that only one window could receive the light of the sun at precisely 5hr.7min, and light up the crib and the infant Jesus."

"It's enchanting. I will come back to see it," says the amazed Amadeo.

They leave the church and make for the refugio, which is an unwelcoming large building without any comfort. The water in the shower is so cold that it is surprising that it does not turn to ice when leaving the tap.

"Brrr!I am not losing my time in taking a shower, Ulké."

"To-day I am on strike – I won't wash!"

Stage 12: from SAN JUAN DE ORTEGA to the OUTSKIRTS OF BURGOS

The cold wakes them up, so they start early.

"Good," said Ulké. *"That gives us a little time before BURGOS. I have some of my old friends the storks, who are installed on top of the church. We shall go and see them."*

After a very pleasant walk on the plateau, a forest of pine and small oak trees reaches the plain. The golden fields are full of poppies, cornflowers, camomiles, buttercups, large thistles, buzzing with insects and black ants scurrying on the ground. The sky is blue and high up the larks are singing.

It is a perfect morning.

The storks have seen them from afar, as their nest on the roof the church gives them a panoramic view

"Good day Madame, I was hardly born when you passed last year. My mother cannot come because she is looking after the last brood."

"Let's go up straight away," says Ulké joyfully.

It was quite a business to hoist Pietre on top of the belfry. Everyone gives a hand, but Pietre does not dare to look down as he has vertigo.

After such a strenuous effort they decide to stay the night. Pietre has attached himself to the big bell, frightened of moving in his sleep and falling down. The others who do not suffer from vertigo find this very amusing.

64

Stage 13: The OUTSKIRTS of BURGOS to BURGOS

They are now very close to BURGOS

"I am going to show you the best view of the Cathedral," says Ulké. *"It is from behind that you will see the beauty of the spires. They are very impressive. The cathedral is enormous."*

The cathedral is flamboyant gothic, and its construction was started in 1221 by Ferdinand the third of Castille. It is so large in fact there are at least fifteen chapels inside.

In a spur of enthusiasm, Ulké flies to the highest spire and describes all she sees.

"It's marvellous – I do wish you could be with me."

Pietre politely declines the invitation.

"It's not for me!

Ulké goes on:

"I can see the Rio Arlanzon, alongside the beautiful public gardens. I can see the Puerta Santa Maria on the other side of the Rio, the church of San Lesme, and further away the monastery of Las Huelgas and at the far end of the park, the Hospital del Rey and the small chapel of San Amaro."

"Get down quickly. I am dying with impatience to visit the cathedral."

They make the tour, going up and down innumerable staircases and eventually they are in front of the magnificent Puerta Del Semental, with its four apostles surrounding Christ on the tympanum.

" So much sculpture and such detail," Pietre finishes by saying.

"I do not know where to look," complains Julius Caesar, my head is spinning.

"Let's do the tour slowly and finish by the chapel of Santo Christo."

They arrive in front of the transept.

"This is the tomb of the Cid Campeador."

"The Cid? Who is he?"

In Arabic the Cid is also "Al Cid", which means the Noble Man or in Spanish "El Campeador". The nation's hero was in fact Rodrigo de Bigard, but very early on he was given this legendary name when the King Sancho ll of Castille named him commander of the royal army. Born in 1043 his life was particularly hectic before he died in 1099.

He started to fight the Moors for the king of Castille, but on the King's death, he did not like his successor, King Alfonso the seventh, and offered his services to King Al Mutamin, who had been the adversary of King Sancho.

Al Mutamin was delighted to have this brave warrior with his renowned sword Tizona in his army against the christian kings. But as Le Cid won all the battles, King Alfonso decided to forgive him and called him back to his side. Yet decidedly they could not get on together and Le Cid returned to the Moors, but this time without fighting Castille, his true country.

Having admired his tomb, they go towards the chapel of Santo Christo

"My god, this Christ looks more real than life," says Amadeo. *"Look how he seems to suffer."*

"It's terrible to see what humans are capable of doing."

They remain along while silent, very moved, and then Pietre looks towards Ulké and says:

"I do not understand. We are always been given humans as an example, but they are capable of such cruelty."

"Its true," says Amadeo.

"Look what they did to Pietre and and even Julius Caesar, tearing him away from his family. It's monstrous."

"But you have not understood anything," said Ulké. *"It is for that reason that Christ has come to pardon sinners with his sacrifice and so they can start again as I might say ...on the right foot."*

"I believe," says the little mouse. *"that all men should once in their life walk the camino 'on the right foot'. This would help them consider the consequences of their acts."*

" It is perhaps for that reason that the Camino has existed for so many centuries."

On leaving the cathedral, they walk under the Arc de Santa Maria. Pietre would like to visit the museum, but Ulké says it is time to go to the refugio at the other side of the rio and at the far end of the public garden.

Under the plane trees which give so much needed shade, there is much animation with children running everywhere as well as students in noisy discussion, laughing loudly. Mothers are proudly parading their new babies, buried beneath multi-coloured ribbons. It is totally charming.

They follow the river Arlanzon, the water being so clear they can see the trout.

"It is beautiful, those pebbles that shine in the sun and the green algae. I would so like to go for a swim."

"We must get our sellos stamped and find somewhere to sleep."

In the refugio, they are welcomed by Jaqueline, a French lady, who has lived many years in Spain, bringing up a large family. Jesus, the guardian, is also there and between them they go out of their way to help all the pilgrims.

"You are lucky, the refugio is not full and we can let you stay tomorrow as well, so that you can visit more of our beautiful city. You should go to see the Casa Del Cordon, where King Ferdinand II and Queen Isabella The Catholic received Christobal Colon after his second long trip."

"The one we call Christopher Colombus, who discovered America? The same man?

"Yes, he was born in 1451 in Genoa in a Spanish Jewish family, of weavers. Cristobal left very young to go to sea. He was even a pirate in the service of the Count of Anjou, this being a proper job at the time. While sailing he heard stories of 'The Terra Incongita' by Paola Toscanelli, a geographer, and from then on he had but one obsession - to discover himself the 'Western road by sea' to India.

The King of Portugal hesitated to invest in his adventure, so he begged King Ferdinand and Queen Isabella to give him the means to make the discovery expedition, in their name. The King and Queen gave him 500 maravédis from the funds of The Santa Hermandad, to which Cristobal added, another 500 maravédis. He was thus able to sail with three ships: the flagship baptised for the occasion La Santa Maria and the two others: La Nina and La Pinta.

Cristobal made four trips, discovering many islands in the Caribbean sea, which under the Papal Bull became Spanish possessions.

Excellent navigator but an exceedingly bad administrator, he made so many mistakes in these new territories that he fell out with the King and Queen, returning at the bottom of the hold with irons on his feet. After a while, the King and Queen forgave him, as it was thanks to his obstinacy that The New World was discovered which brought so much wealth to the realm of Spain.

He died in 1506, one year after Queen Isabelle".

"There is no kitchen in the Refugio," said Jacqueline, "but at the end of the park there is a small inn. Please tell the patron that you are pilgrims."

The patron, a fat and jovial man, received them with open arms.

"Come in! Come in! Pilgrims are always welcome."

After a delicious meal, they return to the refugio, where Jesus is waiting for them.

"Tomorrow - 'café con latte' in my garage., After that, I recommend that you go to mass in the Cistercian monastery, where my sister is a nun and where they sing divinely gregorian chant."

Following Jesus' suggestion, they enter the church by the public entrance. Through the grills separating the public from the nuns, they can see the beautiful tombstone of Alfonso the eighth and Eleonor Plantagenet, their feet on big sad lions.

Alfonso was only fifteen and his queen nine years old when they were married, both dying in the same year in 1214 following forty years of married life.

The nuns enter, all dressed, in white, their hands hidden in large sleeves and with a black veil. The mass begins and the melodious gregorian chant transports our friends into another world.

"I thought I was in Paradise!" said Julius Caesar on leaving.

"The music was so calm and pure that I wanted to remain with them," admits Pietre.

When the nuns had returned to their private quarters, they visit the monastery, which was built by Alfonso the eighth to stay away from the torrid heat of the plains. His wife, Eleonor, daughter of Henry II Plantagenet and Alienor of Aquitaine, Queen of France and then of England asked the king to build a monastery for the young noble women of the aristocracy. The Mother Superior was always of royal blood and had power of life and death over her 'subjects'.

The mother of Eleonor, the Duchess of Aquitaine was, also remarkable and her culture and love of the arts were immense. Eleonor was certainly influenced by her mother, judging by the treasures in Las Huelgas.

They enter a thirteenth century cloister, where there is a ceiling of Mudejar style arabesques, and then a small cloister enclosing a small chapel.

"Look at the statue of Saint Jacques, his arms are articulated. It was in use at the coronation of the king of Castille. King Ferdinand the second thought it unworthy to ask the services of simple citizens and considered the statue of Saint Jacques, being so symbolic, was much better."

They go on to vast rooms, where are exhibited a profusion of weapons, jewels, clothing embroidered with geometric designs and beasts as fabulous as those of the romanesque capitals, all belonging to the royal family of Castille.

"Look at this hat - how beautiful it is – all embroidered with pearls, with the blazon of the king."

"He must have looked great with it."

"We must not stay long. I am sure there are many more interesting things to see, but the Camino is calling us."

Following the yellow arrows, they pass in front of the Hopital Del Rey, which has an enormous dark wooden door, made of ebony. It came from the New World at the time of the Empereur Charles-Quint who reigned from 1516 to 1556. The hospital, was built, for the pilgrims who would find medical assistance, food and sometimes even clothing when the pilgrims were too badly clothed.

Sculpted on the door are images of poor pilgrims hardly clothed, dying of hunger: - A mother with her infant, a father holding the hand of another child and Saint Jacques himself .

"It's strange to see pilgrims of that period. They really had need of a hospital."

"The conditions were extremely hard, and that is why there were so many hospitals along the Camino, thirty-five already in Burgos."

They start walking again, very happy to leave the town behind them.

"It was fantastic, but I still prefer the camino and the countryside," said Amadeo.

"We are at the beginning of La Meseta. At 900m. Nature too can be very cruel. In 1673, an Italian priest, Fr. Laffi found a pilgrim half dead devoured by a cloud of locusts, and was able to give him the last rites before he died."

"Brrr! You frighten me stiff with all your stories. I could almost shiver in the heat!"

They walk one behind the other, on a small path bordered by wild flowers, when suddenly Caesar stopped.

*"From here you can see the earth is round. The horizon draws a huge circle around us. We are in the centre of the worl*d," concluded the mouse, very pleased with himself.

When they eventually reach HORNILLO DEL CAMINO, dying of thirst, they stop at a fountain with a cockerel, made of stone, with multi-coloured feathers.

"How funny it is to recall the legend of the villain pilgrim who instead of thanking the villagers for their kindness tried to steal a cockerel. When the villagers realised what had happened and recovered their cockerel they threw him out."

"He must have been a robber, a thief as you have told us before, not a true pilgrim."

They arrived at the new refugio, recently refurbished, and enjoyed a good dinner with the usual crowd of pilgrims.

Stage 15: HORNILLO DEL CAMINO to CASTROJERIZ

As often in the morning, the sun is shining when they start their walk. Later in the day they cross the Rio Garbazuelo and see the ruins of the convent of San Anton. It was here that the monks cured the disease called,"Saint Anthony's Fire" - a disease very frequent at the time which resembled leprosy. The monks would look after the sick by playing the flute and imposing, them the 'TAU' a cross in form of a T.

They continue their Journey to CASTROJERIZ. All along the camino arrows painted yellow are on walls, stones, tree trunks in fact absolutely eveywhere.

"It is to show the route, so it is difficult to get lost," says Ulké.

Castrojeriz is now in view, but far away and very small in, the distance, right on top of a mountain.

"It is difficult," grumbles Julius Caesar at the end of the day *"to climb so high – my legs are hurting."*

"It is precisely for that reason that the Goth Sigeric choose to build his castle here at 760m. He could see his enemies, arriving from far away and so had time to prepare for their arrival."

At the entrance to the village, they visit a Romano-Gothic church - Our Lady of Apple Trees, built in 1214 by Dona Berengula, who is burried now with Eleonor at Las Huelgas. King Alphonse, the tenth called 'the Wise' wrote hymns about the miracles of the 'Virgin of Apple Trees.'

After obtaining the sellos on their, their credentials, the monk shows them a beautiful painting of a Santiago pilgrim by Bronzino, as well as the tomb of Dona Eleonor queen of Aragon.

"Ulké, please, I can't take anymore. Let's go to the refugio," implores Julius Caesar.

A Spanish couple of hospitaleros, Juan and Carmen, welcomes them kindly.

"Boys upstairs and girls downstairs," says Carmen.

"Oh please, we are used to being together since the beginning of the Camino."

She looks at them, surprised by their appearance and the resistance to her instructions . After a short period of reflection she tells them:

"I can see that you are not ordinary pilgrims. You can stay together."

They wake up the next morning to the delicious smell of grilled toast that the hospitaleros are preparing for the pilgrims. The Spanish pilgrims drench theirs in olive oil in front of the disgusted eyes of the jam eaters!

"Everybody has their own custom!" says Pietre the philosopher.

Stage 16: From CASTROJERIZ to FROMISTA

"From, the windows of the refuge you could see the camino, right up to the next mountain. The rest is hidden," explains Juan. *"Buen viaje!"*

The morning is beautiful. They are very hot as the climb is tough, but fortunately the fresh air is cooling them.

They reach the frontier between the Provinces of Burgos and Palencia, old boundaries between the realms of Castille and Leon. The bridge Fitero on the river Pisuerga separates the two villages: Itero de Castillo is the last Castillan village and Itero de La Vega is the first village of Leon. This very large bridge has eleven arches and was built by Alfonso, the sixth in the twelve century.

During the middle ages;, Abbot Ramon de Fitero founded an important hospital here. He was not only the abbot but also a valiant knight, who with a 2000 strong army defended the Fort of Calatrava against the Moors.

Leaving Boadilla del Camino they find that the church of Santa Maria is closed but they can admire the Rollo Gotico, sculpted with scallop shells from top to bottom.

"You see scallop shells everywhere," notices Amadeo.

"It's the symbol of the Camino"

"It's strange but even when alone on the Meseta you get the impression that you are not really alone, but that thousands of invisible pilgrims are accompanying you."

"It's the magic of the camino," says Ulké. "That's what I wanted you to see."

After walking along the canal of Castille, they arrive at FROMISTA, where the church of San Martin fills them with joy.

"Sorry if I am a bore repeating myself," says Pietre, "but I love these romanesque churches – the simplicity and in the same time the richness of the sculptures with their fantasy and simplicity."

"San Martin was founded in 1066 by Dona Mayor de Navarra."

"Look at these animal heads under the round tiles – they look fantastic."

The inside of the church is even more beautiful with its sculptured capitals and in the plain choir a simple Christ on the cross beside two beautiful statues in gilded wood.

With a flap of a wing, Ulké goes to speak to the pigeons on the rooftop, only just in time before a group of Danish cyclists arriving fast.

"Quick! To the refugio if we want to have a room for the night."

Stage 17: FROMISTA to CARRION DE LOS CONDES

The Danish pilgrims had certainly drunk too much Rossi of Valdepenas. They snored all night, and it was not on the best of form that our friends started again the Camino.

"It's really nice to be by ourselves," sighs Ulké, *"far from this noisy crowd.*

"I'm getting hungry," says Pietre.

"Me too, and I'm thirsty"

"We are nearly in Villacazar de Sirga."

"Look, we can already see this huge fortress church built by the Templar of Santa Maria La Blanca. Inside there are innumerable treasures and a magnificent altarpiece retracing the entire life of Christ."

Amadeo was as always subjugated by the colouring of ancient paintings, and stays there admiring it, while the others discover the splendid tomb of Don Filipe and his wife Dona Leonor.

"That man was huge!"

"Don Filipe was nearly two meters high."

"I will not believe people who pretend that the Spaniards are all short."

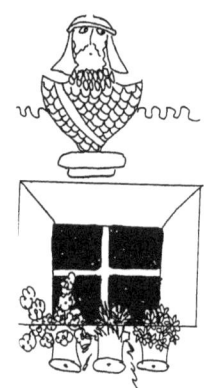

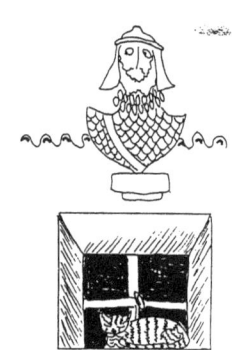

Leaving the church, they went immediately to the restaurant nearby, where the menu was the well known garlic soup with a glass of Valdepenas.

"I am quite pleased to taste it," said Pietre, who has taken quite a liking to the Vino Tinto.

"Yes, but no more than one glass. We are still a long way from Carrion de Los Condes where we shall sleep tonight."

"The Camino is not very attractive here," complains Amadeo – *"straight, always straight in this dusty plain. We were wrong complaining when we were climbing up the plateau, at least the landscape was changing."*

"The Camino is like life! Everyday is different."

"So let's look forward to tomorrow," adds the little mouse.

"To night, we will be in Carrion de los Condes. You will see it is a beautiful town."

In the refugio, which is adjacent to the church of Santa Maria there is a door which leads directly to the church – very practical when it rains. They look at the 'Pancreator Christ' on the Santiago church, which was built in 1106.

"It is a marvel of the eleventh century, and notice how light are the robes of Christ."

"It seems they they will rise with the slightest breath of air."

"The symbol of the Apostles are beautiful"

"Such a pity that the rest of the church was destroyed by the fire in 1809."

They leave to see the Fountain of the Convent of Santa Clara, which is protected by a grid.

"There are many interesting things to see in this convent, but we must return."

The Padre's sister is quite capable of shutting the Refugio's door. In fact she was waiting there with an enormous 'bocadillos de queso', which is the joy of Julius Caesar but not Pietre.

"It's rather dry – could we not have a drop of Vino Rosso?

The Padre's sister gives an indignant chuckle and shows them the water tap.

"You are pilgrims - not tourists."

In a low voice, so that she could not hear, Pietre mutters:

"You can see she does not walk all day long with the wind and dust.

The next morning, they return to the front of the Santa Maria church to look again at the carving on the portal, representing the famous virgins that were handed over to the cruel Calife. It is said that all this happened in Carrion and that is why they are represented here.

Stage 18: from CARRION DE LOS CONDES to SAHAGUN

In leaving the town, they follow the walls of the monastery of San Zoilo, in which are the tombs of the children of Carrion. It is said that Ben Gomez was the rival of the Cid. The Cid, nevertheless, gave the hand of his two daughters, to the Infants. But the Infants tied the young girls to a tree, stripping and abandoning them.

"Scoundrels!" growls the dog.

The Cid, furious, immediately, took his revenge, marrying his daughters to the Princes of Navarro and Aragon.

Carrion was a very importantant city at the time. Many kings lived there: Alfonso the third, Fernando the first, Alfonso the seventh, Fernando the third, Sancho, the fourth and Alfonso the eleventh. It was on this site that the fratricide war between Sancho, of Castille and Alfonso of Leon took place.

They go through an immense area where vast cornfields succeed one another; it is called La Meseta del Plan, and one can understand why. The golden shoots of wheat ripple in the wind, which becomes more and more violent.

"One could believe they are waves in the sea," says Amadeo the poet.
The wind doesn't please Julius Caesar, who is furious.
"Now this cursed wind starts again - I cannnot go any further!"
"We are going to stop in the shelter of these haystacks for our picnic."

"It is queer, despite the blazing sun it's freezing!"
" It's the wind."
"The picnic seems even better when the Camino is difficult," says Julius Caesar, biting a piece of chorizo.

"Now that we are rested its is time to start again … Sahagun is calling us! Let's go, companions."

They leave happily as the wind is less strong, but now dark clouds are building up over their heads. Ulké looks at the sky with apprehension – she knows well the elements.

"I do not like the look of this at all. Hurry up!"

No matter how hard they try they cannot avoid the downpour that falls on them.

"Ah, this is the last straw," says Julius Caesar. My two paws are stuck in the mud. *"Help! Do not forget me!"* he shouts with his small voice.

"Let's go to the macadam road. it will be easier there." Sahagun appears in the distance.

"It's not too early," says Pietre, his teeth clattering with a large drop of rain at the end of his nose. *"I am really cold."*

"To allow you to forget the cold, I will tell you a legend. We are going to cross a bridge on the river Cea. It is said that when Charlemagne was fighting the giant Moor Aigolando, all the spears of the Christian warriors turned into wood, took root and bloomed during the night. The poplar trees by the river are said to be result of this weird story."

At long last they are in the city, but impossible to find a refugio. They are drenched, and finally an old woman takes pity on them and opens her umbrella and takes them to a refugio.

"Gracias – Muchas Gracias!"
"De nada, de nada."

A bad tempered priest, without speaking or smiling points them to their beds. It's a welcome that lacks warmth.

Pietre, who still has chattering teeth, sighs.
"I wonder if I will ever be warm again."
"Do as I do," says Amadeo, getting under a blanket.

Ulké, being the only one not disturbed by the rain, goes into town to find a restaurant, while the others try to get warmer.

At this moment, they hear a strident scream. It is a poor pilgrim who was surprised by the amount of toilet water that flushed on her head.

"Poor girl, she managed to avoid the rain and now she is as wet as we are and shivering, and almost in tears."

"Come to the restaurant with us," says, Ulké to comfort her.

Going to dinner, they admire the twelfth century church, San Tirso of mudéjar style.

"Mudéjar?"

"It is the arab craftsmen who had placed their knowledge and skills at the service of the christian church – hence this particular style."

" Is that why they are made of red bricks?"

"No. It's because there was no stone in the country. Sahagun had been an important city. In 904 a monastery was created by the monks of Cordoba, who were fleeing the Muslim oppression. In 1080, King Alfonso the seventh asked the Cluny Order, who at this time were very powerful through their great wealth and interlectual influence, to reform the ancient monastery. San Bernard of Aquitaine, King Alfonso's confessor, was so successful that there were eventually more than fifty monasteries depending on Cluny in the region, and French was generally spoken."

"Look! what we need! A pilgrim's menu!"

The young pilgrim girl has stopped crying. She was so happy to be among friends for the evening, having been walking alone the last three months, coming all the way from East Germany.

During the dinner Ulké recounts another story:

"Sahagun was known for several great men in the thirteenth century : San Juan of Sahagun the patron of Salamanque; Pedro Ponce of Leon, who was the first to find a way for the deaf and dumb to read and write. In 1530, Brother Bernardino, who found himself in the New World, was horrified by the devastating effects of colonisation. He tried to preserve all he could of the Atzeque world in writing about the Precolumbian civilisation in both Atzeque, Spanish and Latin. He also sketched the Azteque Gods, and the flora and fauna of the 'New Espagne'"

They all return to sleep in the refugio, warmed by a scorching hot soup called 'Olla Podrida'.

Stage 19 : from SAHAGUN to EL BURGO RANERO

The rain has stopped. Very white clouds are in the sky. The day is easy, not like the day before, and they reach Burgo Ranero in good form. After having the sello on their credentials they settle in the superb Refugio.

"It's not like yesterday," notices Pietre.

"The structures and the beams are magnificent. What a good idea to allow one to judge the extraordinary work of the carpenters. Old houses renovated that way are splendid. And look! we have separate bedrooms – what a luxury."

In the sitting room the large book that you find in all the, refugios is open. You are able to write your name and address and eventually share your recollections. Suddenly Pietre exclaims laughingly:

"Listen to this. It is a Spanish pilgrim who is asking Saint Jacques and all the saints to be forgiven for the thousand swear words and blasphemy he uttered against the wind these last few days. It must be the man we came across in Najera."

"Here is the address of a good restaurant: 'Chez Mercedes' – good, I am so hungry."

It's true that Mercedes is a good cook. She too has a book where pilgrims write their thoughts after dinner. Amadeo becomes a poet when talking about grilled trout with bacon. Pietre and Ulké have hardly found enough words to praise the 'alubias con callos'. Evidently, Julius Caesar had his word about the 'queso'.

Stage 20 : From EL BURGO RANERO to SAN MIGUEL DE ESCALADA

The morning walk is long and monotonous, as the camino is straight with very small trees planted every ten metres.

"It will take tens of years before they can provide any shade," grumbles a very hot Julius Caesar.

In the distance, a shepherd with his flock in transhumance comes to meet them and they stop to talk :

"Are you not bored all alone with your sheep along this monotonous path?"

"Bof, I am used to it, and then I am not alone. I have my dog as a companion. In fact I could leave the flock to him and he would guide them to their destination."

They admire his shepherd's staff, ending in a regular spiral.

"How did you manage to do this?"

"It looks like a bishop's mitre"

"Shepherd's secret," he said mockingly. *"I must leave you now as the sheep are eager to find green pastures in the mountains."*

"I can understand," said Julius Caesar; *"I also cannot wait to leave this dreary plain.*

"A bit of patience," says Ulké, *"We will soon be in Mansilla de las Mulas."*

They arrived at the medieval walls, with the river Esla flowing nearby, enter the city and have a picnic in the large square under its wooden arches.

"We have a choice: either we stay the night -- I know a refugio which is brand new, where we would be very comfortable -- or we walk a little further to find a place in a wild and isolated corner with dried grass as a mattress and the sky and stars for cover," says Ulké.

"We stay here, as we have already walked all day," protests Julius Caesar.

"No, no," the other two are indignant. *"If Ulké proposes an alternative it must be worthwhile."*

Julius Caesar drags his feet, furious.

"As if the camino is not long enough like that," he whispers softly for fear that Ulké might hear him.

When they arrive in San Miguel de la Escalada the beauty of the site delights them all. Julius Caesar claps his hands.

"Oh Ulké, you are so annoying – you are always right. This place is wonderful, and it would have been such a shame to have missed it."

"I knew you would like it!"

They sit down comfortably, bocadillos in hand, and listen to Ulké:

"The church was built in 913 and the style is Mozarabic, being the contrary to the churches in Sahagun. Virtually all the Christians living under the domination of the Muslems were influenced by the arab style mosques and palaces and hence the Mozarabic style.

Having finished their frugal meal and drank the water from their gourd, Pietre remarks :

"This would please the sister of the parish church of Carrion de los Condes as we are like the middle-age pilgrims, drinking the water of the river and sleeping under the stars.

Stage 21 : from SAN MIGUEL DE ESCALADA to LEON

"To-day," announces Ulké, "we leave the province of Palencia to enter the province of Leon."

They can already see the town far, far away.

"It is strange, after having slept in such a peaceful countryside to find ourselves on the asphalt, in the middle of noisy and smelly traffic."

The suburbs seem endless.

"The city does not seem to get any closer. We shall never arrive," said the discouraged little mouse.

"To help you pass the time, I will tell you the history of the city of Leon. Leon is one of the oldest towns we shall be visiting, and its name originates from the latin 'Legionis', for indeed in the year 70, it was the camp of the seventh Roman legion Gemina.

In the third century, a centurion, Marcelo, who became a saint, was martyred for his Christian faith, with his wife and sons. Then followed the muslims and 'Legionis' was devastated, being reconquered in 510 to become the capital of the kingdom of Ordono the second. Finally in the thirteen century it was attached, by marriage, to the kingdom of Castille.

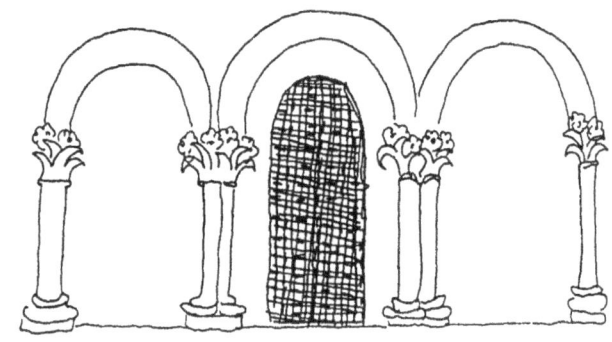

While listening, they arrive at the Castro Bridge over the Rio Torio.

"Look, copper scallops are encrusted on the sidewalk."

"It is the Camino signature," said Amedeo, delighted.

"Let's go to the cathedral right away. Pietre, you who are the great lover of the Roman church, I want to give me your impression."

In the cathedral they are speechless before the splendour, the elegance and finesse of this great stone church. The sun plays through the stained glass windows – its scintillating designs are reflected on the large plilars and the paved floor.

"It's fantastic," says Pietre.

"*There are eighteen hundred square metres of stained glass in this cathedral. It is truly a marvel of Gothic Art.*"

Pietre remains silent in his appreciation. After a while he says: "*Magnificent, and what purity of lines, sense of space, and such lightness.*"

Ulké laughs. "*I am going to make Pietre go crazy. Follow me.*"

She takes them to the church of San Isodoro, and when they are in the crypt they remain speechless, full of admiration, their noses in the air, to look at all the details of these romanesque frescoes that completely cover the vaults of the royal panthéon.

"*I do not know where I am; we go from splendour to splendour.*"

"*Look at these little men who work on the land.*"

"*Yes*", says Ulké, "*it's is according to the season. Here in September, they harvest the grapes. And look at these people, how they sit quietly by the fire, with their bread and wine. It is the result of a year's work. They can rest in December.*"

"*They make me hungry,*" says Pietre.

"*Well,*" suggests Ulké,"*lets go to the Parador San Marco. It is on the site of a former hospital of the Knights of Saint Jacques, built by King Ferdinand the Catholic in 1513 as in Najera. Its style is plateresque. But the most important for us is that the Parador is a hospital for pilgrims.*"

"*Like in Santo Domingo de la Calzada?*"

"*Yes.*"

"*So maybe they will respect the tradition?*"

"*We can always hope,*" says Ulké – "*We must try.*"

At the reception of the hotel, they are not at all well received.

"*You look strange,*" said the concierge, who doesn't want to let them in.

They are saved by the tourists: American, Japanese, Australians, Brazilians who surround them taking photos...

"*Fantastic, marvellous,*" they say in all the dialects of the world. "*Let them in, we will pay for them.*"

It is a beautiful moment of human friendship.

A monk who was passing by said "*Ubi caritas et amore, Deus ibi est.*"

"*What did he say?*" asks Julius Caesar.

"*With your name, you should, understand latin. It means 'When there is love and charity, God is present'.*"

They enjoy to the maximum the luxury of the Parador. Amadeo, who has really changed, disappears in the bath with two doses of bath salts. Pietre opens the fridge and wonders what drink he is going to take. Julius Caesar zaps different programmes on the television. Ulké appreciates the finesse of the duvet.

"*Good quality*, she says knowingly. "*I can understand why humans are mad about them.*"

The following morning, they take a huge breakfast and Julius Caesar discreetly fills his sack with brioches, churros, biscuits, honey, jams and a bit of cheese that they couldn't eat.

"*That is going to make a marvellous picnic.*"

The television, the local newspaper, the tourists, everyone is there in the square of the Parador to wish them 'Buen Viaje'.

"It is not unpleasant to be a star," observes Julius Caesar, swollen by his importance.

"Be careful not to be big-headed," laughs Amadeo.

"I can already see the newspaper headlines: 'A pilgrim mouse obliged to stop on the camino, his head weighing an insufferable weight!'."

Julius Caesar is completely crestfallen.,

"It is not my head. It is the bag on my shoulder."

"You are certainly prudent, It was not necessary to carry all this – we can always find what we need on the way."

Having crossed the Rio Bernesqua, they continue to a village called LaVirgin del Camino.

"This village has a story,", begins Ulké. *"The legend has it that a man from Leon, a captive of the Moors, prayed every evening to the Virgin del Camino for, his release, as a birthday present. On that very day, his Muslim master, sceptic but prudent, had the captive chained and placed in a big coffer on which he sat and fell asleep. He was awakened by the sound of the bell celebrating the return of the captive to his Christian land. As proof of the miracle, the grateful man gave his chains to the Virgin del Camino."*

While listening to Ulké, they arrived at Villalongo del Paramo.

"It was here that in the year 1111, Queen Urraca of Leon and Castille fought, in a battle her husband Alfonso VI of Navarra y Aragon."

"A wife against her husband?"

"Yes, and each at the head of their army. The Queen, who didn't love her husband, fought for her son - a war that lasted 20 years. I will tell you more about Urraca later on – she was a woman of great character.

They are now walking on a plain at the height of eight hundred metres.

"The famous Amairy Picaud from the middle ages said this place was a real desert?"

"Now look at these plantations, it is quite the opposite of a desert."

"But how come?"

"Thanks to irrigation. The water comes from the Rio Luna and, is drawn into these canals."

"Since you told me about the desert, I am thirsty and hungry."

"Let's go inside this cultivated area. We will picnic there with the treasure of Julius Caesar, and stop by the heron."

"Excuse me, Sir. Do you mind if we stay here?"

"Please do," says the heron. "It is a lovely quiet place and I am very honoured to have you staying here. I hope you won't mind if I remain silent – I am meditating."

They swallow, rather too quickly, their lunch, because the presence of the heron intimidates them. They do not dare make jokes as usual in front of this great thinker.

They resume their walk towards ORBIGO.

"You will see a huge bridge over the river Orbigo. It is two hundred and four metres long and has twenty arches. It is very famous and is called The Paso Honroso de Armas, and it also has its own story."

"Tell us!"

"In the year 1434, Don Suero de Quinones, who passionately loved Dona Eléonore de Tovar, wanted to draw her attention. With his friends, nine knights from Leon, he launched a challenge to all the knights of Europe, that they would never be able to cross the bridge. The tournament lasted a month – three hundred spears were broken and one knight died. The victors went to lay a gold necklace as an offering to Saint Jacques. Twenty four years later Don Suero was killed by a knight, with whom he had battled on the bridge."

"And the lady?"

"It is unfortunately not known if she fell in love with him."

They dine in an inn, gazing dreamily at the bridge. It is crazy how things looks different when you know the history. The bridge is not just a bridge – it is THE BRIDGE.

"I hope the ghost of the dead knight won't be here," said Julius Caesar, shuddering.

"I would not mind to see the ghost of Dona Eleonore and to ask her if she had succumbed to the charms of Don Suero."

"Let's sleep. Tomorrow we are going to ASTORIA, and you will see an extraordinary Roman wall."

Stage 23 : from HOSPITAL DE ORBIGO to ASTORGA

The morning walk is pleasant. The weather is fine, the vineyards have reappeared and the grapes are ripe. In each vineyard, one can see a whole family at work. The old women are in the shade, preparing a good lunch. Seeing them pass, a grandmother calls out :

"Hey Peregrinos! Ven aqui, come here, I'll give you some bunches of ripe grapes."

The grape pickers, curious, quit their work and come to have a closer look.

"Pilgrims are always welcome," says the father of the family, after observing them for a while. *"We are not rich, but if you want to share our meal, you are most welcome."*

In the stream, the bottles of last year's wine are cooling, sausages roast over the fire of vine shoots releasing a delicious smell and potatoes cooked under the ashes are ready. Everyone sits by the fire. The conversation is lively as each member has someone of his family working abroad. They know some words in all the european languages and it is fun to try to pronounce them. Julius Caesar, encouraged, spells out his little Spanish vocabury.

"Me llamo Julio Cesar, y mi gusta mucho el queso."

It is very successful! The grandmother gives him a large piece of cheese.

"Thank you, but I am not hungry anymore," he says regretfully.

"I see you have a bag. Put it in there for later."

"Ah, Julius Caesar's bag," said Pietre, who carries it so often.

"What would we have become without Julius Caesar's bag!"

At last they have to leave. Everyone kisses with promises to give news.

"Do not forget to pray for us in Compostela."

They can see in the distance the spires of the cathedral of Astorga.

"Astorga is a city even older than Leon," Ulké recounts. *"It belongs to prehistory. This is said of all early periods of history where there are no documents but only archaeological evidence that certain people lived there. Here in Astorga, the prehistoric inhabitants were Astures and Amacos. When the Romans invaded, they named Astorga 'L'Asturica Augusta'. It was very important for them, being the crossing of roads from the North and the South: La Via Triana coming from Bordeaux and La Via de la Planta coming from the South. It was the Romans who built the great walls that you can still see."*

"It's amazing. The walls look brand new!"

"Yes, the Romans were such good builders that we can see their presence throughout Europe and even Africa."

They pass the town hall, at the very moment when the bell of the clock starts chiming. Two small model Maragates armed with large hammers bang the bell with all their might.

"How pretty they are!"

"Yes, they wear the regional Maragato costume. Everyone argues about their origins – some say they are Berbers and others that they are Asturies who resisted the mutiple invaders and knew how to preserve their traditions."

"I hope they are resistant Astures. It reminds me of Asterix the resistant Gaul," says Pietre laughing.

"Maragota people still live here," adds Ulké.

They continue their journey towards the gothic cathedral, built in 1471, and admire the beautiful porch of Baroque and Renaissance style with Saint Jacques dressed as a pilgrim.

"What I like most about this cathedral is the little fellow on top, carrying a flag," says Amadeo, looking up.

"It's the statue of Pero Mato, a hero of the battle of Clavijo. It is said that a piece of his standard is still kept in the Town Hall."

Leaving the cathedral, they walk towards the Gaudi Palace.

"What is this?"

"It's neither Gothic nor Roman."

"You are right. It is neo-gothic or modern."

"It is the work of the famous Catalan architect Gaudi, who built this palace in 1889 for the bishop of Astorga."

"It doesn't look real."

"Come inside, it is even more extraordinary."

Amadeo once again remarks on the sun shining, through the stained glassworks making beautiful patterns.

"Look at all those spiralling staircases – like in an ancient dungeon of fortified castles. This place is a cross between a palace and a church, and you have not seen yet the museum with all the statues of Saints and its Jacobite and Roman steles."

It is time to go to the refugio to have their credentials stamped, The refugio is run by Dutch monks, who also have a school nearby. It is not very clean, despite an impressive number of little boys armed with brooms sweeping in all directions!

"The good fathers have certainly instilled a sense of Christian duty and Charity to their pupils, but have forgotten to give them a sense of practicality. They sweep without collecting the dust," observes Pietre, sneezing.

"Let's go ouside under the Roman walls, until they have finished cleaning."

Stage 24 : from ASTORGA to RABANAL DEL CAMINO

It is a superb morning with blue sky. They leave early as after the Meseta they will start the climb on approaching the Montes de Leon.

"Ah! This walk is different," says the delighted Julius Caesar.

They pass through many ruined villages.

"We are nearly there," says Ulké.

"What a pity! All these deserted houses."

"Yes, isn't it sad. These are Maragatos villages. Previously very rich mule drivers lived here, and, they had plenty of work. Now that all the trucks and lorries take the road, nobody has need of their services anymore."

They continue to climb up the mountain.

"I am still happy to have left the Meseta, but I will be delighted to arrive," says Julius Caesar, out of breath.!

"I can see the church and nest of one of my friends. Let's go quickly to the Refugio. It is completely new and appears to be splendid. It is run by the brotherhood of Saint James."

"Why Saint James?"

"Saint James is Scots for Saint Jacques."

The hospitalero who receives them is a former Commander of the British Navy.

"'In one row', he told them when they presented their credentials.

"This document contains the 'Rules', and you must respect them. You can now go to the dormitories – lights are switched off at ten o'clock."

"Pfuitt!" whispers Pietre. *"It might be splendid, the English refugio, but I will not stay here longer than necessary."*

"Come to the village inn," says Ulké, laughing,*"but be careful not to tell the Commander, if unfortunately it is against the rules!"*

The inn at Rabanel is wonderful. The whole village is there. Some play cards, others follow passionately the end of the football match and on another television, others cry 'ole' at each pass of a brave torero. In the kitchen, the cook sings 'le bel conto' with his bass voice, aided by a radio diffusing Carmen. At the bar, the old customers recount the recent misdeeds of the youngsters.

"*The shower is cold,*" complains Julius Caesar.

"*It is indeed, so that the pilgrims do not forget their condition and that, too, shapes their character,*" says Pietre with a sigh.

At six in the morning the Commander bursts into the dormitory, turning on the lights.

"*Come on, you, have ten minutes to get up. Breakfast is ready.*"

All the pilgrims, so used to being pampered by the hospitaleros, are very astonished. In fact, to be a hospitaleros, you are obliged to have completed the camino yourself, which generally creates a certain empathy with the pilgrims.

Despite everything, the breakfast smells, and is actually very good: coffee, chocolate, toast and when the Commmander tells them to wash their plates,"*It is the rules*" they comply, giggling!!

Stage 25 : from RABANAL DEL CAMINO to MOLINASECA

They leave so early that the mountains are still shrouded in morning mist. The summits in the distance form a blue line on the horizon, while the nearest hills stand out in a palette of green of every imaginable shade. The bells of a herd of honey-coloured cows echo in the distance, and in the pastures bushes of wild berries line the Camino. It is happiness!

"Thank you, Mister Commander, to have thrown us out of bed at dawn," cries out Julius Caesar. After all the military virtues are not to be despised.

They walk through ruined villages. It is desolate and sad with so many houses almost completely destroyed. A yellow letter box gives an incongruous note of colour .

"Who can use this letter box other than stray dogs and wild chickens, as I cannot see anyone around?"

"Well, you are wrong!"

Indeed, a little further down the road, a flock of geese are caqueting.

They are invited to go to a tiny refugio that a former pilgrim created in this remote corner of the mountain. Transported by the beauty of the landscape he stopped there., For him the camino adventure was over and he would never see Santiago. But in order to remain in some way faithful to his ideal, he helps, especially in the winter, pilgrims passing by.

They enter a kind of shambles. There are thousands of postcards and documents of all sorts about the Camino, partitions of music, Saint Jacques shells, old empty cans, plates, rickety furniture and also and most important of all – a coffee pot that simmers on the fire, all accompanied by divine gregorian chant. The bearded and hairy hospitalero who welcomes them is a member of the Templar's Order. He serves a cup of very hot coffee and tells them that during winter it can be very hard here as the snow is always abundant and the freezing winds are dangerous for the pilgrims.

It is soon time to start again.

"Can you the imagine the Commander's face in front of such a mess?"

"He would not find that it is according to his regulations," puffs Pietre laughingly.

The camino climbs up and up. It's getting harder and harder.

"Courage, we will soon be at 'the Cross of Ferro' at 1490 meters altitude," says Ulké.

"Pick up a stone," she tells them. *"We will place it at the foot of Mount Joy. This is an old tradition."*

Having placed their stones on Mont Joy, they remain a while admiring the range of mountains. They are now at the highest point of the camino and will descend to the village of El Acebo. This village is very rich, as in ancient times they were not paying taxes but in return they had to plant wooden posts in the snow to avoid the pilgrims getting lost. They are now walking through wonderful countryside. The houses, with uneven slated roofs and their wooden balconies crumbling with flowers, are peaceful. Here and there streams rustle, as if accompanying the chirping of larks high in the sky.

"What beautiful music," whispers Pietre. *"It is even more beautiful than gregorian chant."*

"It is said that the monks only transcribed in their chant the sound of the wind in the mountains and the song of the birds in the sky. Their music was inspired by nature and that is why it is so pure and peaceful."

The camino now meanders on the flanks of a hill, covered with shrubs.

"Mmm! How good it smells!"

"It's those fruit and sticky leaves that produces this delicious smell."

"It smells like incense."

"Oh, it sticks to the paws," says Amadeo, who breaks off a branch.

An old shepherd, who was passing by, said that he makes herb tea with this to make men strong.

"I do not know if he has drank any, but he has not a single tooth left," notes Pietre. *"That smell goes to my head. I feel drunk!*

They continue their walk to Molinaseca.

"I said I would tell you more about Queen Urraca. In fact, on the other side of this Roman bridge, over the Rio Meruelo, you can see her house. But I have a surprise for you, so let's go down to the bridge."

They scream with pleasure as, a little below, a swimming pool has been built by the river and all the children of the village are gathered there.

"We will see if Amadeo remembers his swimming lesson!"

When the children see them, it's delirium. Amadeo, glad to show that he fears nobody, makes leaps and dives that will remain in the amazed memory of the inhabitants of Molinaseca.

"This bathe has made me hungry! Wait for me and I will try to find something to eat before dinner," says Julius Caesar, who having searched his bag, found it hopelessly empty.

He returns triumphant with a large cake box.

"It's great," he shouts from afar. *"The lady who offered me this cake lived for twenty years in a street behind where I lived in Paris. She gave us all a big Parisian style pear tart and refused any payment, just saying 'Pray for me in Compostela'."*

"It's a jolly good pie, ' says Pietre, licking his lips., With his tall thin body he is always hungry.

They cross the long main street where strange smoke escapes from the dark openings of the houses. Men and women come out surreptitiously. Large quantities of grapes disappear inside.

"What are they doing?" asks Amadeo.

"If you are asked, say that you do not know," advises Ulké.

They arrive at the end of the town, where there is a small modern refugio with a adorable hospitalero, Juan, a student who, like many of his friends, dedicated three weeks of his holiday to the service of the Camino.

The refugio is full of pilgrims of different countries; Juan proposes to cook a huge dish of spaghetti. Gedeon and Andreas, two young Swiss students, who had walked from the door of their house in Zurich, are very willing to help. Fortunately, there remains some pear tart for the dessert.

"Sehr gut, sehr gut – French pastry!!"

Stage 26 : From MOLINASECA to VILLA FRANCA DEL BIERZO

For breakfast, Juan insists everyone takes a clove of garlic, a ancient Jacobite tradition. He talked severely to the pilgrims who tried to avoid it; his eyes are laughing.

"After, I will give you whatever you want – croissants, brioches, but I will not take the responsibility of letting my pilgrims go in this dangerous world, unprotected against the thousand microbes that await them at every turn of the road."

Juan is a medical student.

It is raining 'cats and dogs'. Juan hands out plastic bags as protection, and the pilgrims look like astronauts, but our friends refuse this protection.

"I am too small," says Julius Caesar.

"I do not fear the rain," adds Amadeo.

They are soon in the suburbs of Ponferrada. The rain has stopped. They are almost dry when a truck overtaking them splashes them from head to toe.

"What a brute," says Julius Caesar, half suffocated by the violence of the splash.

"I am all dripping," says Amadeo, furious. *"Ah! it is not the Maragato mules who would have done this."*

"Let's go to a café to get rid of all this mud and enjoy a good chocolate," suggests Ulké, laughing at his sudden fury. *"After that we will visit Ponferrada. The city is so named, because in the twelfth century there was an iron bridge, being an incredible invention for the middle ages, when all the other bridges were made of stone or even wood."*

They arrive at a medieval bridge, with Roman arches over the Rio Boeza.

"This bridge is no different to the others!"

"This one is. – It is only when we shall leave Ponteferrada and cross the Rio Sil that we will pass across the famous iron bridge. In the mean time, shall we visit the Templar-Castel. King Fernando the second of Leon had left the city in their hands, asking the Templar to fight the Moors and protect the pilgrims?"

The size of the fortified castle leaves them dumbfounded.

"It's terrific – look at all those high towers, the machicolation, it's stupendous!"

"I can imagine the knight in armour, entering on horseback, his banner raised to the sound of trumpets. What a spectacle."

"The knights stayed for almost two hundred and thirty years, but they became so powerful that the kings, becoming afraid ot their power, expelled them from all his territories. It was the same in France, when King Philippe le Bel seized their immense fortune, and these brave knights , who had served him so well, were excommunicated.

They leave the city without visiting the beautiful church of Nuestra Senora De La Encima. The road is still long to Villa Franca del Bierzo, but it is with great pleasure they pass through the vignobles of Bierzo.

"We must not leave the Province of Bierzo, without tasting its wine," says Pietre seriously.

They stop at Cacabelos, and to Pietre's great pleasure, taste a glass of wine.

"It is to compare with the wine of La Rioja," he says.

"I feel that after Compostela, you will make a pilgrimage to the cathedral of Reims to compare the different champagnes and, their tiny bubbles!!

Ulké feels worried as the palms of her feet begin to swell again.

"Fortunately it happens at this stage, as the next hospitalero we are going to meet Jesus Rato, who is a bit of a sorcerer. He will certainly heal me with his herbs, as well as the hospital did.

Arriving at Villa Franca Del Bierzo they pass in front of the door of El Perdon.

"In the middle ages," said Ulké who is now limping,*"I would be able to stop here. For if you were ill, you only had to pass this door to consider that the pilgrimage was finished. But I will not cross it, she said proudly. El senor Jesus Rato will heal me, and I will be able to continue."*

The Rato's family refuge is very strange – enormous, with old military tents, matelases and metal beds placed haphazardly. The walls of the tents are open in certain areas, forming natural windows or large open holes through which one can see the magnificent castle of the Marquis., Built in 1490, it lost its towers during the Napoleonic war.

"Napoleon and his troops caused so much damage in Spain. It was the English who helped the Spanish chase the French out of the country."

The Rato's family has installed solar panels for hot water.

"*Hot shower in such a place. It's miraculous!*"

"*From the look outside, I would not have believed it.*"

"*Long live sun and ecology!*"

In the evening in the large dining room, it is the fiesta and the pilgrims, who are getting to know each other, meet around the large table. Coming from several continents, they look to find a common language.

Jesus is heating a mysterious drink. In turning off the lights some blue flames, are escaping from the pot. Jesus whispers strange words, and all those who understand Spanish burst out laughing.

"*I will certainly learn Spanish*," says Julius Caesar, annoyed not to have understood.

But good humour is contagious, and he laughs with everybody. Jesus finally ladles the drink into a glass and it is handed from hand to hand around the table. "*We have been doing this for fourteen years. It is our tradition.*" He then ladles again further glasses and gives to all the guests, and everyone toasts his neighbour.

"*I do not know what it is, but it is jolly good. I would not mind another glass,*" says Pietre, always ready for a new experience!

Then Jesus Rato examines Ulké's feet, putting some compresses made of herbs picked in the morning dew, the day when the moon wanes.

"*With these compresses and my drink, you will sleep like a baby, and tomorrow you will have new feet, 'Word of a sorcerer'* he said laughing.

It was true. They are awakened to sound of gregorian chant.

"*It's nicer than the Commander's bugle,*" says Amadeo!

"*Come and have a good breakfast,*" says Ulké, who is happily dancing on her healed feet. "*The day ahead is going to be rough, as we shall climb up to 1300 metres, to the crest of Cordillere Cantabrique, being the border between the Provinces of Castille y Leon, and Galicia.*

After hearty farewells, the pilgrims separated in small groups, disappearing into the nature.

Stage 27 : from VILLAFRANCA DEL BIERZO to O CEBREIRO

They pass in front of the church of San Francisco, then the convent of the Anunciada, in which is found the pantheon of the Marquis, and walk down Calle del Aqua, a beautiful street with emblazoned houses, bordered by two palaces

"It is a real shame to go so fast, but the camino is terribly hard to-day and we cannot stop and visit."

After a while they follow the Rio du Valcarcel, passing villages which are hundreds of years old, farms built of dry stones, slated roofs, shaded by chestnut groves. Everything is calm and peaceful.

On leaving the river the camino becomes very narrow, bordered by dry stone walls. They have to walk in a single line, advancing with great difficulty. Large rocks block the way, wild bushes grow everywhere, and nobody speaks. You have to look where to put your feet.

Suddenly they arrive at the top of the crest, and then exclaim :

"What a view!"

"It's stupendous!"

"All these multicoloured fields. It looks like a Persian carpet!"

"Look at the cows. They are no bigger than ants!

Pietre, who is watching, feels suddenly very ill. He does not want to look any more. He feels dizzy, his paws are trembling and he has turned green.

"I shall be delighted to arrive," he moaned. *"I am afraid of falling in the void.*

Paralyzed by dizziness, Pietre can no longer move. Amadeo takes him by the arm and guides him gently.,

"Calm down," says Ulké. *"We are almost there. I can see the steeple of the Church."*

"All for the better," says Pietre piteously.

The tiny village of O Cebreiro awaits them, perched at 1300 m at the top of the Cantabrian Cordillera, being the natural border between the 'brown' Castille et Leon and the 'green' Galicia of Celtic influence.

"Oh!" says Pietre who is feeling so much better, *"Look at these huts!"*

These are Pallozas, prehistoric huts of the Celts. They have survived centuries, like the traditions of the Maragates. One can find them on the shores of Brittany and even in Cornwall, being coastal countries that the valiant Celtic sailors had invaded with their fantastic drakkars.

"Prehistoric huts?"

"Yes, and not so long ago, these huts were still used by the inhabitants of the village! Tonight we are going to sleep in one of them. It is now a Refugio. In the meantime, let's go and visit the church., Its foundations date from the 9th century, when Alfonso Vl entrusted, the monastic church to the monks of Cluny, and where is found the Chalice of the Miracle."

"What? Another miracle?"

"It is said that during a great storm around the year 1300, while everything had disapeared under the snow, a shepherd of the village of Barxamajor came, never the less, to attend mass. The monk, who was evil, inwardly mocked the shepherd:

" 'How stupid he is! Making this trip in these conditions, for a little bread and wine!' Immediately as he had these impious thoughts, the bread and wine turned into flesh and blood!"

"Oh! My God!"

"And what did the monk do?"

"History doesn't say. But the relics of the Miracle are still kept, in the village."

"Here in O Cebreiro?"

"In fact, the catholic Queen Isabella and King Ferdinando passing through here in 1486 were so impressed by the holy relics that she had built a special reliquary to house them. Queen Isabella even wanted to have the relics taken away to avoid leaving them in this little church, lost in the wild mountains. But the mule that was to transport them, being usually very obedient, absolutely refused to move. The Queen thought this was a sign. The relics remained in O Cebreiro and one can still see the chalice and and plate used by the monk.

After admiring the the chalice and the beautiful Virgin, they left for the pallozas.

Julius Caesar remained behind, and kneeled before the Virgin:

"Beautiful Lady, you who is the Mother of all mankind could you also take care of a little mouse? You see, we are almost in Santiago de Compostela. Ulké is going to join her family who are waiting for her in Africa. But for Amadeo, Pietre and me, no one is waiting for us anywhere. What are we going to become when Ulké is gone? Could you not ask the good Saint Francis of Assisi, who had also made this pilgrimage to take care of us. It seems he does understand our kind very well. I thank you in advance for your intervention."

And Julius Caesar gets up to join the others.

When he gets inside the pallozas, he barely distinguished Ulké and Pietre and doesn't see Amadeo at all.

"It's so dark! What's that shining on the left?"

"It's my eyes, idiot! Don't you know that cat's eyes are shining in the night? Come here; follow me, I will put you on this bench."

"But how can I follow you if you turn your back, you are all black in the dark."

"Come on, give me your paws, I'll lead you. There, you will be fine."

"I will go up there in that little niche, lt's just my size!"

"The winter must have been so very long in these huts!"

"I hope people were telling each other stories, as you do, Ulké, to pass the time."

"Surely, stories of goblins, fairies, miracles. Wagner, the great German composer, was so impressed by what happened here, that it was an inspiration for his opera 'Parsifal'. But now we should try to sleep."

"It's a bit hard for a bed," growls Pietre.

"Think of all the people who, from prehistoric times to the present day, have preceded you and slept here! They had to put up with it. Try to do the same!"

"Ouch! Ouch!" Pietre grumbles, "I feel all rusty, whatever you say. Ulké, modern confort is great, these stones benches are very uncomfortable!"

"Well, I slept very well! I had a terrific dream, I fought a prehistoric mouse, that had wings like a dragon, I fought like a lion! It was an epic fight!"

"Don't you think it was only a bat. I saw some last night at nightfall."

"Oh!" said Julius Caesar, very disappointed. "You may be right."

They descend slowly but steadily. The mountain is still just as beautiful. Suddenly, at the bend in the road, they see a very large bronze statue, representing a pilgrim struggling against the wind.

"Look, he is dressed as in the middle-ages, with his cape and his round hat."

They sit down to admire the view. The vast horizon is swept by gusts of wind.

"I understand why the artist has made him hold his hat! It's difficult for me with this wind to stand upright!"

Then they take to the Camino again. It continues to descend. Sometimes it winds through chestnut woods, that are so dark that the sun barely pierces through. Streams appear and disappear under large mossy stones, then the forest gives way to pastures. Low walls surround herds of cattle impatient to go to the farm. They pass through Tricastella, the afternoon is sunny and the hollow and shaded path sometimes reveals extraordinary landscape. At the bottom of the valley, they can see the roofs of the Samos monastery

"Let's stop here," Ulkér suggests. *"We're in Triacastela. We can picnic here. What's in your bag, Julius Caesar?"*

Samos has existed since the seventh century, but it has often been transformed. It was a very important cultural center with a wonderful library. Unfortunately in 1835 during the "Spanish demortization Law", bagfuls of very rare and irreplaceable books were sold to peasants who could not read, and were used for lighting the fire!

"Oh," says Amedeo, scandalized,*"Were they illuminated scrolls?"*

"Certainly, a quantity of masterpieces!"

"And it all went up in smoke?"

"Unfortunately, yes ... and the worst is that everything which had escaped that disaster ended up destroyed in a fire in 1951.

In Samos until the eighteen century, pilgrims could stay for three days in a row and share the monk's life.

Having visited the monastery, certainly very restored, they find themselves in the cloister, where an extraordinary fountain catches their eyes.

"What are those? Sirens?"

"Those are Nereids, half women half fish."

"The result is not successful," says Amadeo, who turns around them.*"They are ugly, They should be at the bottom of the ocean."*

In the large dormitory, they find all their friends from Villafranca del Bierzo.

"When we left Roncevalles, we were just four of us and now we have plenty of friends," said Pietre, before falling asleep.

"Wonderful Camino! And friends from all over the world!", adds Ulké.

Stage 29 : from SAMOS to PORTOMARIN

They walk on happily. The sky is all blue again; the Camino continually crosses many hamlets. Cows, behind their granite walls, wish them 'buen viaje'. Each farm has curious little constructions placed on large stones.

"What are those?"

"Those are 'horreos', small granaries where the corn is dried," explains Ulké.

"They are raised on those big stones to keep nasty mice like you from devouring the entire crop!" says Amadeo, laughing.

They pass through Sarria without stopping. It is here that King Alfonso the IX of Castille died when he was doing his pilgrimage. They continue their walk chatting, and after an abrupt descent, they see a large expansee of water.

"Oh, a big lake!"

"No, it's not a natural lake; it was caused by the dam on the Rio Mino. Imagine that! A whole village is engulfed on the bottom."

"My God! And the inhabitants?"

"A new village was built for them on the heights. They even rebuilt stone by stone their old church of San Juan dating from the thirteenth century, a fortress church of the brother of St John of Jerusalem."

They cross the bridge, and look curiously at the roofs of old houses, that they perceive under the water. It is strange and it gives the feeling of a ghost village.

After a stiff climb they arrive at the church.

"I can't believe it," says Pietre, turning around. *"It gives the impression of having always been there!"*

"It was a big job, all the stones had to be numbered in order to be able to reconstruct it."

"What a work!"

"It was worth it. It would have been such a shame if these sculptures were lying at the bottom of the lake."

"Look at the Christ Pancreator, surrounded by the 24 old men of the Apocalypse."

"I would, love to play on beautiful instruments like these!" says Pietre, with a sigh.

"And I would like to know how to sculpt like that," replies Julius Caesar. *"Look at this Blessed Virgin, and the angel, and this little stone tree! We want to climb it!"*

"What I would like is to paint with beautiful colours like all those Renaissance painters," adds Amadeo. *"And you, Ulké?*

"All I have left is dancing," she giggled. *"And my height, and my feet, are not the best suited for this magnificent art! Let's get our credentials stamped at the refugio and have dinner at a bar."*

The small bar is filled with peregrinos. There are plenty of delicious things to eat. Amadeo, always fond of fish, takes sea fish à la "Gallego", Jules César and Ulké, the "Gallega" hotpot. Pietre says to his Belgian neighbour, who is speechless in surprise: *"I recommend the 'Empanada'; the crust of this pâté is delicious! I am licking my chops."*

122

Stage 30 : From PORTOMARIN to VILAR DE DONAS

In crossing the Belesar reservoir again, Julius Caesar is very excited. He points out the remains of the old bridge that shows on the surface.

"This bridge was built in 1120 by a certain Pedro Peregrino, and he would be very surprised to see it under water, as it is today. It is amazing to think how this landscape has been so transformed since 1962."

Pietre the music lover says *"It is reminiscent of a work by Debussy - 'La Cathedrale Engloutie'."*

Ulké says: *"I will talk about Queen Urraca. It is here on Portomarin that she had a bridge destroyed to prevent her second husband, Alfonso VII of Navarra, from entering Galicia, her own territory."*

They climb up the hill overlooking the river. There are vines and fields following one another, surrounded by granite walls on which a golden brown moss draws strange geographical 'maps.' The old farm houses with dry stone walls, uneven slate roofs seem to have been there since the dawn of time. A smell of cow's dung floats in the air. Small vegetable gardens, with their blooming sunflowers and fig trees crumbling under their fruit, show to anyone who could doubt it, that the silent farms are indeed well inhabited.

"These figs look very appetising," says Julius Caesar.

"Do not touch them. The peasants here are very poor and all their harvests are important to them."

At that very moment, an old man carrying a wicker basket stops them.

"Hola Peregrinos!"

"Hey, Senor!"

"Take these figs – they will give you strength to get to Santiago," he said with a broad toothless smile.

"Gracias, muchas gracias, but we do not want to deprive you," says, Julius Caesar, craving to taste them.

"We always help Peregrinos. It is our tradition and our pride," says the old man.

They all take a fig.

"Muchissmas gratias, Senor!"

"Buen viaje! Pray for me in Compostela."

"We will indeed. It is the tradition," answers Ulké.

They continue to zigzag through a now deserted countryside, until they finally see Vilar de Donas.

"Donas means 'noble ladies', as it was two noble ladies from Galicia who in the thirteen century built this church and hospital., What a pity it is in such a bad state .One has the impression that it is sinking into the ground, but the porch is still very beautiful."

"Have you seen the St Jacques? He holds the 'Bourdon' in one hand and his sword in the other, managing to be at the same time; Santiago and the Matamoro."

"Let's go inside."

"Brrr— It's cold and the frescoes are all damaged."

"It's caused by the humidity, but we can still recognise the frescoes of the two Donas, who built the church."

"And these tombs?"

"They are the knights of Santiago, who always had the same mission, that is to drive the infidel out of their country and protect the pilgrims."

They continue to admire all the damaged treasures of the little church.

"It's really too cold. I am going outside," said Pietre, shivering.

"Let's go up the hill to those big oak trees where we will camp to-night."

In the wood, there is a gypsy family, near a beautiful Renaissance house.

"Hola!"

"Hola! Peregrinos?

"Yes, we are going to Santiago."

"We are going back to Sainte-Marie-de-La-Mer, for the great meeting of all the Gypsies," said an old gypsy. "If you are not afraid, come and sit with us."

Amadeo asks "Why should we be afraid?"

"Oh, it is very usual – everybody is suspicious of gypsies."

"Everybody is wary of black cats – so we are quits," Amadeo smiles, amused with himself.

"The world is stupid," said Paquita, a lovely gypsy brandishing a wooden spoon. "You are invited to taste my cooking. On the menu: trout that Miguel has fished in the river five minutes ago, with mushrooms that I picked myself and peppers and artichokes my grandmother prepared."

Then it is a real fiesta. Without understanding what happens to him, Amadeo finds himself on the gypsy's lap and she caresses him. It is the first time in his life that such a delightful thing happens to him."

"You are so handsome!"

"Do you think so? The farmer said I was hideous."

"Nonsense!"

"I draw cards for you. Hum, hum!, I see plenty of good things: a house, a boy, a girl. For the moment the little girl I see is crying., I see the sea, fish and a lot of work."

"But how do you see all that?"

"It's in my cards, you idiot. I am a bit of a witch as I am a gypsy," she said, laughing very loudly.

"Ah, that's why you find me handsome. The farmer who hated me called me 'son of a witch'!"

"So you see, birds of a feather flock together. It takes everything to make a world."

Meanwhile, Pietre is captivated by the sounds that Manuelito produces on his guitar. He is accompanied by the trill of a blackbird, which punctuates each verse with: 'Manuelito muy bonito!'

"He is my best student!", he said proudly pointing to the blackbird.

"He is so lucky," says Pietre. "I would also like to study with you and know how to play the guitar as well as you do."

"Here, have a try. I will show you the first chords."

After a while Manuello said how gifted he seemed to be.

"Dinner is ready," sings Paquita. "Come around me!
They all enjoy the meal to the last morsel.

"It was delicious," says Julius Caesar, licking his fingertips.

"Come on; the festivities are not over. Now let us have a lesson of Sevillanas!"

Amadeo, who has not exhausted the joy of being caressed, remains lazily on the gypsy's knees. Ulké and Julius Caesar prove to be very talented dancers, but not the same for Pietre who is as stiff as a broomstick. The night is full of stars. The moon rises and falls in the sky. The fire is no more than a heap of embers. It is time to go to bed.

Stage 31 : from VILAR DE DONAS to ARZUA

Pietre's compliments on his music went to Manuelito's heart. *"Here,"* he said, *"take this guitar. It will be a souvenir of our meeting."*

"Oh, I can't. It is too beautiful."

"Yes, yes ... gifts keep friendships alive and the next time we meet I absolutely want to dance to the sounds of your music."

Pietre has tears in his eyes. *"I promise I will be very careful with it."*

After several warm and noisy Adios, they take to the Camino again. It is still very hot and in crossing the Palas del Rey, they dive into a fountain. Julius Caesar has climbed on top to talk to Saint Jacques.

"Santiago, listen to me. I am afraid the Camino will soon be over. Saint Francis of Assisi must have told you about us. What are we going to become?"

While cooling off in the fountain, Ulké tells them: *"Palas de Ray is a very old town. Its name comes from the latin 'Palatium Regis' and it was in 701 the city of a Visigothic King called Witiza."*

Leaving the fountain, they start again the Camino.

"It is funny," said Amadeo, *"we are very close to Santiago and I am eager to arrive but at the same time I wish our trip would never end."*

"It is the same for me," said the little mouse with a small voice.

"Yes; I hope we will find a good solution for you," said Ulké, preoccupied. *"I would feel terribly sorry to have brought you all this way if it was not for your happiness."*

"Oh, please do not worry about us. The three of us are extremely grateful to you and also to have known the Camino."

"Oh yes," said Amadeo, *"we have learned so much about the world and the men who live there."*

A river meanders lazily in the middle of green meadows. Farms are pretty with their decorated 'horeos' and the geraniums give out their rich bright colour. Women wash their linen in the river and strike it vigorously with their beaters. The children gather the washing to spread it out on the rocks to dry in the sun.

"Look how beautiful it is," says Amadeo.

"Yes, we are lucky to walk this part of the Camino in the sun, as seeing how the grass is so green, it must surely rain very often."

Soon the woods through which they travel become a forest of eucalyptus, at first sparse then becoming more and more numerous and then entirely replacing the oak and pine trees.

"How pretty their foliage is!"

"What delicate green," says Amadeo, always sensitive to colour. *"And it smells so good."*

"It is with the leaf of the tree that the eucalyptus candy is made to ease the harmful effects of winter."

"Oh look here, this tiny shelter made of huge granite slabs with a strange little statue inside."

"It looks like a pagan prehistoric statue, yet his hands are joined together as if praying."

"Stop a second —this statue intrigues me, and it is lucky to be protected from the sun."

The path is so narrow that they have to pass in a single line.

"And what is that?

"Oh, it's rather sad, as it is a monument in memory of an old American man who died of exhaustion one day before completing his pilgrimage."

"How sad!"

"His family had his walking shoes cast in bronze so that the more fortunate pilgrims passing by could remember him."

"He died like a pilgrim of the Middle Ages."

"He was not the only one. In the village of Acebo, the family of a cyclist who had died had his bicycle and gourdon cast in bronze as a memorial."

"Now that we have seen this memorial I am more than eager to arrive in Santiago."

They leave the province of Lugo to enter
the province of La Corunna, where the city of
Santiago is situated. They pass through Melide
and Arzua but as they are so keen to arrive
they do not make any more visits.

"I have counted," said Pietre, *"that to-day
we have seen ten different rivers and three
beautiful crosses."*

*"It is because of all these rivers that the
region is so green. To-morrow, before arriving
in Santiago we will be at Lavacolla and will
respect the tradition. I will tell you about it
during the last stop.*

*But tonight we shall be like the ancient
pilgrims, and sleep outside and have something
to eat."*

It is a frugal meal – dry bread and a few
olives, but enhanced by Pietre's music who has
retained Manuelito's tune in his ears.

"It is really different from last night," says
Amadeo, who is above all missing the gypsy's
caresses.

"It's good," says Julius Caesar, for once
reasonable. *"We shall appreciate Compostela
even more.*

Stage 32 : from LAVACOLLA to SAINT-JACQUES DE COMPOSTELLE

They awake at dawn. The sky is still pink and the birds are singing to the top of their hearts. Silvery clouds look like a flock of sheep, and dewdrops shine like diamonds.

"Amadeo, you have a drop of dew on your moustache!"

"And you on your ear!"

"I am a little cold," says Pietre, *"We are missing the gypsy's fire.*

"Let's go," said Ulké. *"Lavacolla is far away and we shall bathe there."*

"A bathe?"

"Yes, and I will tell you why. In the middle ages, when the pilgrims arrived at last in Lavacolla after all their tribulations, they were filthy, covered with louse and vermin. Hot showers were not available like for us modern pilgrims. And so, not to contaminate the population of Santiago, it was customary that they undress completely and wash themselves and their clothes in the Rio. They could then appear in front of Santiago without either shame or scratching themselves!"

They arrive in front of a pretty stream with a crossing of large mossy flagstones.

"What a wonderful bridge!"

"Of all the bridges I have seen, this is the one I prefer," says Amadeo, darting nimbly from one stone to the other.

"Yes, it might be romantic but I am too small. Help! Do not leave me behind," cries Julius Caesar, panicking.

The brave Pietre turns and helps him across the Rio.

There are hamlets that follow one another and then the camino, bordered by magnificent trees, digs a deep furrow in the forest.

Pietre is standing in front of an enormous chestnut tree.

"I wonder," says Pietre,*"how many pilgrims, passing by, have seen this tree? It must have seen the very first pilgrims."*

"You are joking?"

"No, there is a chestnut tree in Sicily on Mount Etna, which is almost four thousand years old. It is so famous that it has even a name: 'The Chestnut Tree of One Hundred horses'."

"This one would have seen so many civilisations: prehistoric, Greek, Roman, Visigoth, Aryan, Muslim and Christian."

"It's incredible!"

"But nevertheless true."

"The four of us with our legs and wings can't even get around it," said Pietre admiringly.

"It is such a pity that this tree cannot speak."

They arrive at the "Monte del Gozo".

"In Latin it is 'Mount Gaudi' and in French 'Mont-Joy'. It is so called because from this mountain at 368 metres you can see Compostela."

"The Mountain of happiness! What a name!"

"If the pilgrims could arrive this far, it was already a miracle! Then there was a race to reach the top and see Santiago de Compostela, and the first to arrive was declared the king. He took such a pride in this that very often he changed his name and called himself 'The King'.

"And where is your Monte del Gozo," ask Julius Caesar, innocently.

"There in front of you!"

"Forward Santiago!" shouts Julius Caesar, rushing forward with all his might.

The others, taken by surprise, can't join him in time. Even Pietre with his big legs has trouble standing because he laughs so much. Amadeo collapses head first in the grass, Ulké tries to cheat and fly to the top, but could not get rid of her staff and gourd in time.

"I am the king! I am the king," exclaims Julius Caesar

"No doubt you are the king!"

"With your name, you were predestined to rule," said Pietre, laughing.

When they reach Lavacolla, they are bewildered.

"It can't be true!.. Look at the runway and all those planes?"

"Where is the Rio?

"I guess unfortunately that it is the tribute of modern times. No doubt they could not have done otherwise."

"We will look further for the Rio Lavacolla."

"Yes. I want to respect tradition at all costs."

Amadeo is the first in the water.

"Are my ears perfectly clean? What about my back, I can't see it. I would hate to arrive in Compostella looking a mess."

"And me, is my fur really white?"

"Yes, Sir, your majesty is superb."

Ulké meanwhile tries to smooth her feathers.

The dog shakes unceremoniouly after his bathe. He is ready and waits patiently for the others. They are now all clean and feel they can make a dignified entry into Santiago. Leaving happily the traffic and the modernity of the oustkirts of the city does not weaken their ardour.

Pietre remarks: *"I am sure it is the only part of the Camino that the elders would not recognise."*

A dark cloud that they had not noticed becomes suddenly menacing, and before they realise what is happening the sky is falling on their heads. They are soaked from head to toe.

"Hardly worth trying to be presentable," fulminates Julius Caesar. *"I am all muddy!*

"It is is typical of Galicia," says Ulké, philosophically.

ARRIVAL at SANTIAGO-DE-COMPOSTELA

They enter Santiago, through the Baroque-styled streets, whose granite façades sparkle with mica shards under the sun, which has at last broken through the clouds.

It is really crowded everywhere.

Children in uniform hurry so as not to be late for school, students and businessmen have their last morning coffee in bars. Housewives hurry towards the market where a multitude of fruit and vegetables catch the eye. The restaurants, with their windows filled with molluscs of all kinds, are amazing .

"By God, it all looks so appetising," said Pietre.

"We will come back later," the others say impatiently. *"Quick! Let's go to the Cathedral."*

"Oh look—on the wall there is a representation of Santiago arriving on his boat."

After having been a bit lost, they arrive at long last at the Plaza del Obradoiro and are speechless.

"Ah, I was expecting something grandiose, but it is even more splendid than I thought it would be."

"It is even more beautiful than I ever imagined."

After a few minutes of contemplation an irrepressible joy takes over them. They begin to dance, holding each others' legs and wings, chanting *"We have made it! We have arrived!"*

The tourists, always present, begin to surround them, but they are not in the mood.

"Oh! No! Not today, leave us alone."

"We must go now and present our credentials and obtain our 'Compostela'."

"Ah, finally," said the priest who welcomes them. *"I have been waiting for you for a long time., Fortunately news travels faster than pilgrims. I am curious: tell me why did you make the pilgrimage?"*

Ulké tells him briefly how she found her little companions in distress and, knowing the reputation of Santiago de Compostela, she thought of making the pilgrimage.

"Admirable, admirable, what a wonderful story. We shall take your photo for the local newspaper as we do for all pilgrims who are of special interest."

The priest carefully chooses his best stamp for the credentials, already well filled in, and taking his pen makes the most elegant signature possible.

"There you are," he said. *"This will be a wonderful souvenir of your joint venture. Now go to the Monastery Minor, a school where the top floor is reserved for pilgrims. You will be able to sleep there and have a splendid view of Compostela. The Hostal de Los Reyes Catolicos provides food for the first ten pilgrims of the day. It is a beautiful Parador, and you should try to go there.*

Tomorrow, at high mass, we will exceptionally ask you to help with the Botafumeiro. We do not do this very often, but you pilgrims are out of the ordinary."

They return to the Plaza Del Obradoiro. They want to reach the cathedral by the magnificent steps of the porch. On the left is the Hostal de los Reyes Catolicos of the early sixteenth century, and on the right the seventh century San Jerimino Del Artista college and the Rajoy Palace built from 1766.

"Ulké, tell us about the Cathedral."

"The facade," says Ulké, always compliant, *"is from the eighteenth century in a baroque style and designed by Casas y Novos in 1738."*

"This man must have been an optimist to have imagined such a building."

"And not suffer from vertigo," emphasised Pietre. *"Look at the height of the towers!*

"What you see here" continues Ulké, *"is in fact the third church to have been built. When the remains of Santiago were discovered by the Hermit Pelayo, the cruel Queen Luppa was asked to lend her bulls to transport these relics to a safe place. The wicked Queen, who abhorred Christians, lent her wildest bulls. She was so surprised to see her ferocious ungovernable bulls becoming as gentle and obedient as lambs. She realised it was a miracle and converted immediately to Christianity.*

The news of the miracle of Santiago spread very quickly across Europe, and the initial chapel became too small to receive all the pilgrims. A large church was built in 889.

But the Muslims, who were ruling most of Spain at that time, came to destroy the entire church with the exception of the Apostle's tomb. The Moorish king El Mansour, to mark his disdain, made his horse drink in the baptismal font, and forced the captured Christians to carry the heavy bells of the church on their backs to the city of Cordoba, being, at the time a great cultural Muslim centre."

"Oh! Depriving a church of its bells is to make it mute."

"It was exactly what El Mansour intended. But history can be strange. In the thirteenth century it was the moorish prisoners who brought these same bells on their backs to Compostela.

It was finally in 1105 that the construction of the present cathedral began, and was almost completed by 1128. From pure Romanesque at the beginning, each century, brought its touches of different styles, including the most beautiful addition 'the Porch of Glory' by Master Mateo in 1188."

"You are right, Ulké, its incredible!"

"How beautiful the Christ is!"

"Why is he so much taller than the others?"

"The artist wanted surely to signify his superiority as the son of God. Each of the apostles has a distinctive sign."

"The eagle is magnificent. It looks like our friends on the Camino!"

"What are these angels doing with the cross?"

"They carry the instruments of the Passion."

"Look at the wise old men of the Apocalypse," said Pietre, very excited. *"I am sure they are going to give a wonderful concert. They look in such a good mood. One could imagine they are telling jokes to each other, while waiting to play their music."*

"You would like to be with them," says Julius Caesar, laughing.

"No," said Pietre,*"I am still a very bad musician."*

"Look at this young man, surrounded by these bearded men. Why is he laughing like that?"

"It is the prophet Daniel. It is said he is smiling to Saint Suzanne, who is on the other side of the porch."

"Now listen to me," says Ulké. *"The middle column represents the Tree of Jesse. This is the family tree of the Virgin Mary and consequently of her son Jesus. The dove at the top represents The Holy Spirit and the old man is God The Father. Above all these symbols it is Santiago himself who welcomes us."*

"What are those holes that the pilgrims are touching?"

"They say this is the handprint of Master Mateo and if you make a wish while putting your fingers in the little holes you obtain the grace you have asked for."

"But why did you not say this earlier?" said the little mouse rushing forward, *"I have a lot of requests."*

"You also have to place your forehead against the statue of Master Mateo if you wish to benefit from his ideas."

Having performed all the traditional gestures, they enter the Cathedral, wandering around, happily looking at everything. They have a feeling of being at home, free from the harassment of ordinary life and to have gained through sheer perseverance a great interior strength.

"I feel so good," sighs Julius Caesar. *"I do not know why, but right now I am no longer afraid of the future."*

"What wonderful peace, and at the same time what extraordinary agitation. Everyone comes in and out, talks and laughs aloud."

"It does not seem to disturb those who are praying," notices Amadeo.

"It is because a church is really a house and this house belongs to all these men of goodwill who came from all over the world."

"Even if they are not catholic?"

"Sure, many of the pilgrims we met on the Camino were not catholic, some even claimed to be atheist. But for all this, it is their house. For example: look at this man who told you the other day that he didn't believe in anything, and particularly not in God. Look how happy and peaceful he looks now compared to his usually tormented face."

They are now in the choir of the cathedral, and after having admired the wonderful organ, they head towards the back of the altarpiece where a small staircase takes them behind the statue of Santiago. They are obliged to stand in line as there are so many pilgrims waiting their turn. They then pass with either a paw or a wing around the neck of the Saint to touch the cross of the pilgrimage.

"See you to-morrow, Santiago," whispers the little mouse, *"and listen carefully to your friend Saint Francis of Assisi.*

"Let's go down to the crypt to see the reliquary of Santiago."

"It looks so small."

"It is because the remains of the Saint have changed place so often that they were all broken and were eventually restored in a silver reliquary. In 1589 the Archbishop Juan de San Clemente hid the relics, frightened by the venue of Francis Drake. The English Pirate had a bad reputation of looter. The location of the hiding place was forgotten until February 1879 when it was discovered, yet again."

"Let us hope that this time it is there for good."

"You told us we could see the gold necklace of Don Suero de Quinones," recalls Amadeo. *"I want to see it before we leave the Cathedral."*

"So we have to visit the treasure in the chapel of Las Reliquas."

"It is such a pity that we will never know what happened to the Dame of his dreams."

Amadeo is subjugated by the beautiful necklace.

It is now time for them to go to the last refugio. In leaving they pass in front of the Holy Door. There are some more sculptures of Master Mateo, They represent the old prophets and the apostles.

143

"Why is this door closed?"

"It is only opened on the 31st December, the year preceding the Holy Year, when the feast of Santiago falls on a Sunday."

"What is that?" says Julius Caesar, showing with his paw the signs engraved in the stone.

Ulké explains: *"They are signatures. In the middle age the workers were travelling, from one country to another., When they had finished their work, they used to sign their name in a corner - each workman having his own sign. It was a practical way of knowing who had worked there, and also an indication of the many sites in the country where they had been working."*

They cross the city again down a strange street, where there were no houses but only tall walls on which are carved scallops – old relics of ancient time. They climb a few steps to get to the convent of Santa Maria, admiring the facade, and continue the journey to the Seminario Minor.

They have a huge success with the young pupils of the Seminario.

"Where do you come from? You are so different from the other pilgrims!"

They answer willingly to the young children, who do not know how to believe their eyes. The children take off their meagre parcels, drag them away with loud cries and howls of excitement up a large staircase leading to a huge dormitory. The children argue among themselves as which bed they choose. They select four in front of the windows, that look out over the city.

"What a splendid view," exclaimed Ulké.

"It gives the same feeling as flying."

Pietre does not say anything. He has turned green in one second.

"Pity, Pity! I did not come all this way to have my bed in such a place. It would be quite impossible to go to sleep here."

"Dizziness – he suffers from vertigo," says Amedéo softly to a young boy.

As soon as he said this, Pietre's bed is moved to the least pleasant corner of the whole room – all dark, with no view and turned towards the wash basin.

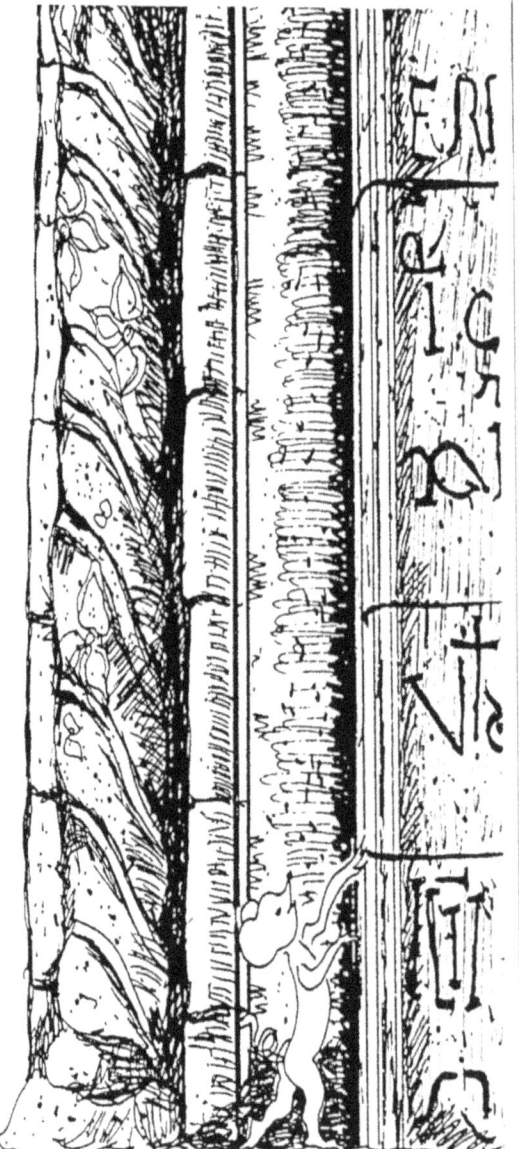

"Perfect! I will be fine here," says Pietre happily, in front of the astonished boys. *"Thank you. I feel really well now."*

The next day they are awakened by the young boarders, even more excited if possible than the day before. They hold some newspapers.

"Look, look! The four of you. You are all in it, and it tells your story!"

"The photos are a good likeness," says Julius Caesar, swollen by his self importance.

"Will you sign your names as a keepsake?"

"Of course we will, but let us first get up and wash," says Amadeo, who has taken a liking to his morning ablutions.

When finally they are ready, they leave autographs on dozens of newspapers. The children are delighted, having permission to go to mass at the Cathedral.

"In the paper it is mentioned that you are going to operate the Botafumeiro. We want to be there."

While waiting for the mass to start, they visit the Museo del Pueblo Gallego.

"What an extraordinary staircase," says Amadeo, always sensitive to beautiful things.

"It is called The Caracol staircase."

"Caracol?"

"It is a snail in Spanish."

"It is true that these spirals are very much like a snail's shell. The true intention of the architect was to indicate by the triple spirals of the staircase the triple ascent of the body, soul and the spirit.

"I am the spirit," says Ulké laughing, flying suddenly to the top.

It is now time to go to the cathedral. A formidable gathering of tourists awaits them, their newspapers under their arms.

"Here they are! Here they are!, they shout, mad with excitement, in their different tongues.

It is even worse than yesterday with the children.

The Japanese, being too small behind the Scandinavians, are crawling between their legs on all fours. A tall Belgian fails to knock out an even taller German. A small Italian argues with a Greek mama who has stepped on his toes. Camera flash continuously!

Fortunately the children are there who act as their bodyguards.

They finally enter the cathedral and the tourists become calm and regain their dignity.

Still accompanied by their troop of children, they enter the sacristy where they are entrusted with the Botafumeiro.

Pietre puts in a great dose of incense. Ulké and Julius Caesar and Amadeo pull with all their strength on the thick ropes. Then the magnificent censer is pitching and gently sailing, a slow curve at first and then faster and faster. The crowd of pilgrims follow the majestic journey of the Botafumeiro with their eyes, and spontaneously stand up and applaud loudly.

All the memories of the Camino, the tiredness, the pain, the joy, the friendship made by chance encounters, the anonymous passers-by who helped them and who had aided them and who asked 'Pray for me in Santiago', all this jostled in their heads.

Julius Caesar prays very hard:

"Santiago, and you Saint Francis of Assisi, do not forget I am counting on you."

The priest goes up to the pulpit and begins to read the names of the pilgrims who arrived the day before:

"We are going to say this mass with a special mention for Uilkje and Pietre from Holland, Andre from Pau, Papychette and Peter from France, Marion and Mario from Canada, Anne from Switzerland, Gedeons and Andreas from Bern, Juan and Manuel from Granada, Guillermo from Brazil, Philip from Austria. But above all let us not forget our famous Jacobeans, OH!, Excuse me! Our 'Jaco-animals' Ulké, Pietre, Amadeo and Julius Caesar. I would like to add to the latter that they should go to the sacristy after the mass. With the help of the Lord a happy issue will perhaps fulfill the wishes of these valiant pilgrims."

Hearing these words, Julius Caesar almost collapses with emotion.

"Oh! Saint Francis of Assisi, and you, Santiago, it's no joke, you heard me. I don't know what will happen yet, but I thank you very much for it. in advance."

Amadeo, Ulké and Pietre look at each other, rather surprised, wondering what will happen.

The mass is over and our friends rush to the sacristy, where a whole family is waiting for them – a grandfather, grandmother, the father and mother, and particularly three grandchildren. Seeing them the father said:

"We learn from the newspaper that you do not have a home. Neither do we, as we were living abroad when a terrible earthquake completely destroyed our house. Thank goodness our lives are safe, and we intend to start all over again here in this country. My parents own an old farmhouse in ruins near Cape Finistera. If you like the idea you are welcome. The children are so sad to have left all their friends behind and a cat and a dog would be most welcome."

The father seeing the unhappy face of Julius Caesar, immediately said:

"Of course a little mouse as well, far from my mind the idea of separating you."

Turning towards Ulké :

"You and your family will always be welcome to stay with us.Each year you will tell us about your travels."

Anxiously, the children are waiting for an answer.

Julius Caesar, Amadeo and Pietre jumped for joy. They are so happy,

"Yes, a thousand times yes."

Julius Caesar is drunk with joy.

"Thank you, thank you again," then, calmed down, he turns to the father. "You will not regret it."

That same afternoon, Ulké made her last walk to accompany them to the ruined house. It is important that she should know where she can find them for her annual trip.

"The house will be very different when you come back. We are going to work hard," says the father.

"This will not prevent us from enjoying the countryside and the sea," adds the mother with a smile.

"That I am sure," answers Ulké. "If it was not for my family worrying about me, I would willingly have stayed behind and given you a hand.

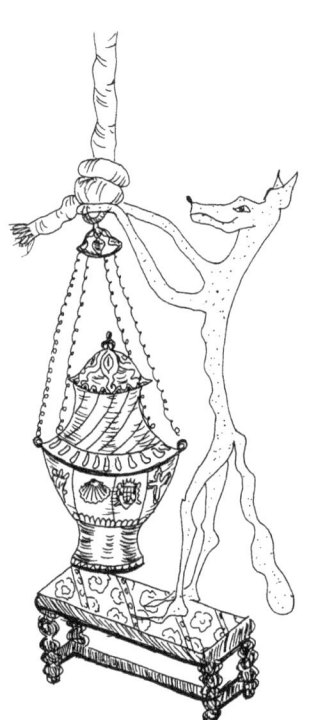

Very early the next day our four friends are heading for the sea. Pietre, Amadeo and Julius Caesar, their throats knotted with emotion and tears running freely down their cheeks, looking at the great wild goose taking its majestic flight. She makes a last salutation and disappears faraway behind the horizon.

"Lets go back," says Pietre in a gruff voice. "We have work to do."

150

The Pilgrim's Passport - the Credencial del Peregrino

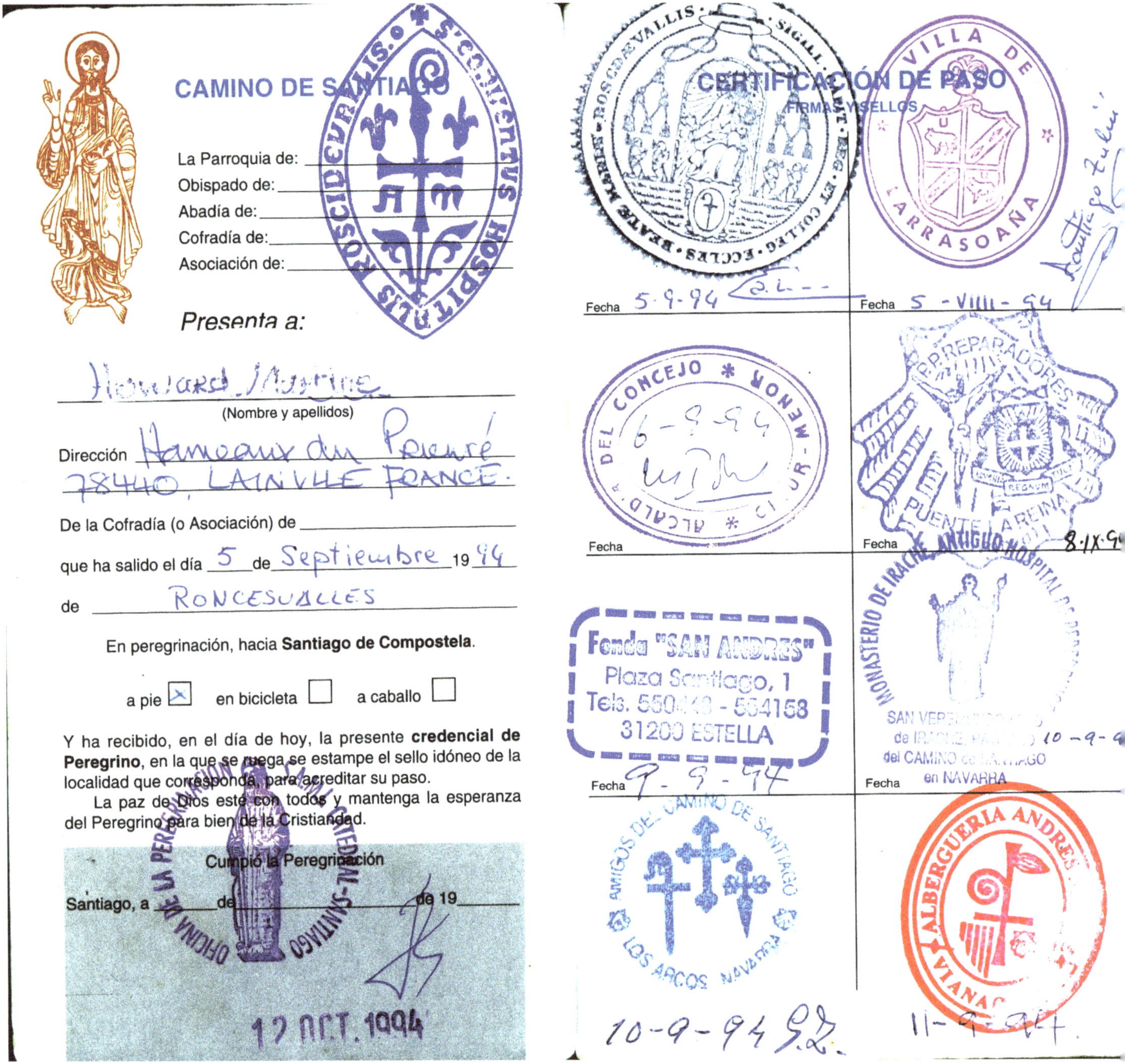

CAMINO DE SANTIAGO

La Parroquia de: _____
Obispado de: _____
Abadía de: _____
Cofradía de: _____
Asociación de: _____

Presenta a:

Howard Martine
(Nombre y apellidos)

Dirección _Hamoaux du Prieuré_
78440, LAINVILE FRANCE.

De la Cofradía (o Asociación) de _____

que ha salido el día _5_ de _Septiembre_ 19 _94_

de _RONCESVALLES_

En peregrinación, hacia **Santiago de Compostela**.

a pie ☒   en bicicleta ☐   a caballo ☐

Y ha recibido, en el día de hoy, la presente **credencial de Peregrino**, en la que se ruega se estampe el sello idóneo de la localidad que corresponda, para acreditar su paso.

La paz de Dios este con todos y mantenga la esperanza del Peregrino para bien de la Cristiandad.

Cumplió la Peregrinación

Santiago, a ____ de _____ de 19 ____

12 OCT. 1994

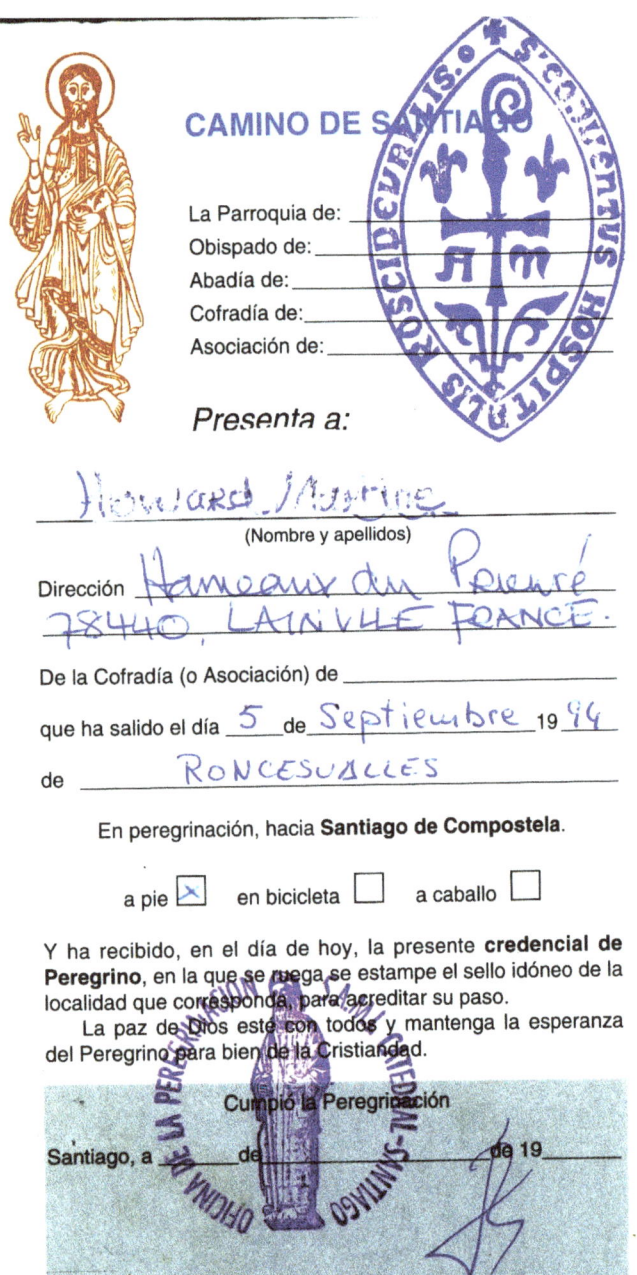

Fecha 5-9-94

Fecha 5 - VIII - 94

Fecha

Fecha 8-1X-94

Fonda "SAN ANDRES"
Plaza Santiago, 1
Tels. 550148 - 554158
31200 ESTELLA

Fecha 9 - 9 - 94

Fecha 10 - 9 - 94

10-9-94

11-9-94

154

FIRMAS Y SELLOS

FIRMAS Y SELLOS

ASOCIACION RIOJANA DE AMIGOS DEL
CAMINO DE SANTIAGO
ALBERGUE DE PEREGRINOS
Tel. 260234 - LOGROÑO

Fecha 12-SEP-94

Fecha

Fecha 15-9-94

Fecha 18-9-94

Fecha 14/9/94

Fecha 14/9

Fecha 20-9-94

Fecha

Fecha 14-9-94

Fecha 15-09-1994

Fecha 17-9-94

Fecha 22-9-94

15-09-94

18-9-94

155

FIRMAS Y SELLOS

CAMINO DE SANTIAGO · CASTROJERIZ-BURGOS

ARCIPRESTAZGO DE CASTROJERIZ (Burgos)

Baudilla del Camino · MUNICIPIO · JACOBEO

AYUNTAMIENTO DE LA MUY LEAL · CAMINO DE SANTIAGO (Palencia) · VILLALCAZAR DE SIRGA

FIRMAS Y SELLOS

Fecha 21-9-94   Fecha 21-9-94   Fecha   Fecha 23-9-94

PARROQUIA DE STA Mª LA BLANCA · VILLALCAZAR DE SIRGA

PARROQUIA DE Sta. Mª del CAMINO · CARRION de los CONDES (PALENCIA)

Hospedería "CAMINO REAL" · Bar Restaurante · CALZADILLA de la CUEZA (Palencia)

Fecha 22-9-94   Fecha 23-9-94   Fecha   Fecha 24-9-94

ILTMO. AYUNTAMIENTO DE SAHAGUN · OFICINA DE TURISMO · TEL. (987) 78 11 12

EL BURGO RANERO (León) · CAMINO DE SANTIAGO

B A R AVOCES · Teléfono 31 05 09 · RELIEGOS (León)

MUSEO

Fecha 25-9-94   Fecha 26/9/94   Fecha   Fecha 9-9-94

MANSILLA

Año Jacobeo · León, 1993 · Oficina de Turismo

CAMINO DE SANTIAGO · AMIGOS del CAMINO de SANTIAGO · HOSPITAL de ORBIGO (León)

Amigos del Camino de Santiago Astorga

22-9-94   29-9-94 Dep   30-9-94   1-10-94

156

CAPITULUM hujus Almae Apostolicae et Metropolitanae Ecclesiae Compostellanae sigilli Altaris Beati Jacobi Apostoli custos, ut omnibus Fidelibus et Peregrinis ex toto terrarum Orbe, devotionis affectu vel voti causa, ad limina Apostoli Nostri Hispaniarum Patroni ac Tutelaris **SANCTI JACOBI** convenientibus, authenticas visitationis litteras expediat, omnibus et singulis praesentes inspecturis, notum facio: _Diane Martineau Howard_ hoc sacratissimum Templum pietatis causa devote visitasse. In quorum fidem praesentes litteras, sigilo ejusdem Sanctae Ecclesiae munitas, ei confero.

Datum Compostellae die _12_ mensis _Octobris_ anno Dni _1994_.

Secretarius Capitularis

Some companions on the way

Papychette on The Way

All the team

Peter, Ulké and Pietre

Papychette

Peter

Meal break on The Way

Valerie in the refuge

Milton Keynes UK
Ingram Content Group UK Ltd.
UKHW050635020124
435306UK00004B/86